LIVING THE
DREAM

IDENTIFYING, CONNECTING WITH
& NURTURING YOUR DESTINY

LIVING THE
DREAM

IDENTIFYING, CONNECTING WITH & NURTURING YOUR DESTINY

By

BISHOP DARRYL S. BRISTER

LIVING THE DREAM: IDENTIFYING, CONNECTING WITH & NURTURING YOUR DESTINY

Darryl S. Brister International Ministries
P.O. Box 1526
Harvey, LA 70059-1526
Phone: (504) 283-8787
Fax: (504) 283-1423

ISBN 1-880809-18-4
Printed in the United States of America
© 2003 by Darryl S. Brister

Legacy Publishers International
1301 South Clinton Street
Denver, CO 80247
www.legacypublishersinternational.com

Cover design by: David Uttley, UDG DesignWorks
www.udgdesignworks.com

1 2 3 4 5 6 7 8 9 10 11 / 09 08 07 06 05 04 03

CONTENTS

≒⊹⊹⊱

Joseph had a dream.
Genesis 37:5

INTRODUCTION

The poorest man in the world is the man without a dream, and the most frustrated man in the world is the man with a dream that never becomes reality. I'm certain that every individual on this planet—no matter what race, culture, nationality, or status he or she happens to be—has a dream of some sort. The ability of children to dream is a natural instinct instilled by the Creator, and as we grow older, our dreaming should never cease.

Dreams are visual manifestations of our purpose, seeds of destiny planted in the soil of our imaginations. I'm convinced that God created and gave us the gift of imagination to provide us with a glimpse of our purpose in life and to activate the hidden ability within each of us.

Purpose is the reason something was made. It is the end for which the means exists. Every manufacturer produces a product to fulfill a specific purpose, and every product is designed with the ability to fulfill this purpose. In essence, the potential of a product is determined by its purpose. This is true of everything God created—including you and I.

The purpose of a seed, for example, is to produce trees. Therefore, by God's design, seeds possess the ability, or potential, to fulfill this purpose. But just because a seed has the potential to produce a forest doesn't mean that it will. One of the greatest tragedies in nature is the destruction of a seed or the isolation of a seed from the soil. Consequently, the death of a seed is the burial of a forest. Having ability is good, but failing to use ability is sin.

Everything in creation was designed to function on the simple principle of receiving and releasing. Life depends on this principle. What if the plants refused to release the oxygen they possess, or if we human beings refused to release the carbon dioxide we produce? The result would be chaos and death for the entire planet.

Unreleased potential is not only useless, it's also dangerous— both for the person or thing who failed to release it and for everything that lives with them. When potential is kept, it self-destructs. You must understand that your valuable deposit of potential was given to enrich the lives of others. It must be used for that purpose, or your life will be spent in continual frustration.

The first chapter of Genesis gives an account of Creation, the creation of the birds, of the creatures of the sea, of the livestock, and of other creatures of the land. These were all given the ability to reproduce according to their kinds. Everything that God created was blessed with potential, and the Source of it all is God. If the book of Genesis had started with Genesis 1:0, it would read, *"Before there was a beginning, there was God. Before there was a creation, there was the Creator. Before anything was, He existed."* God did not begin when the beginning began. He was in the beginning before the beginning even had a beginning.

Introduction

Then, God didn't put the first man in his place until He had prepared the man for the place. There is, therefore, a preparatory process, a learning process, that God takes us through so that we can become the sons and daughters He has destined us to be. One of the greatest problems we're having today is that we want everything fast or faster. We want instant success, instant ministries, instant careers, instantly mature marriages, and instantly mature children. But preparation takes time, and though the process may be painful and revealing, it is, nevertheless, necessary. Think about it. You know that it takes longer to prepare a good meal than it does to eat it!

Now, how does all of this relate to you and me? Anyone else would have given up on us, but not God. Most people are not committed to our forming, but He is. And the tools He uses to mold us are the experiences of life. We're still under construction. When He is finished with us, we will have become beautiful vessels. Until then, we have a lot to learn.

Bishop Darryl S. Brister
New Orleans, Louisiana

Chapter One

LEARNING TO GO
AFTER YOUR DREAM

Now Joseph had a dream, and he told it to his brothers; and they
hated him even more.

Genesis 37:5

"Joseph had a dream." That doesn't sound like a bad thing, does
it? And yet his brothers hated him for it. There was, of course,
more to the story than at first meets the eye. This hatred on the
part of his older brothers had its roots in other circumstances.
Bear with me as I lay a foundation for it, so that we can understand more fully what was going on in Joseph's life:

> *Joseph, being seventeen years old, was feeding the flock with his*
> *brothers. And the lad was with the sons of Bilhah and the sons of*
> *Zilpah, his father's wives; and Joseph brought a bad report of them*
> *to his father. Now Israel loved Joseph more than all his children,*

because he was the son of his old age. Also he made him a tunic of many colors. But when his brothers saw that their father loved him more than all of his brothers, they hated him and could not speak peaceably to him.

Genesis 37:2–4

So the brothers already disliked Joseph, and now he had suddenly become a dreamer. With this, *"they hated him even more."*

To compound this problem, Joseph unwisely told the dream to his brothers, perhaps because they were involved in it, or perhaps because he was still young and unwise. Whatever the case, it was told:

So he said to them, "Please hear this dream which I have dreamed: There we were, binding sheaves in the field. Then behold, my sheaf arose and also stood upright; and indeed your sheaves stood all around and bowed down to my sheaf."

Genesis 37:6–7

This idea infuriated the other brothers:

And his brothers said to him, "Shall you indeed reign over us? Or shall you indeed have dominion over us?" So they hated him even more for his dreams and for his words.

Genesis 37:8

Things were getting worse for young Joseph by the minute. Now, as if he needed more problems, he had another dream, and again it was about his brothers. This time it also included his parents. Unwisely, he decided to tell them all about it:

Then he dreamed still another dream and told it to his brothers, and said, "Look, I have dreamed another dream. And this time, the sun, the moon, and the eleven stars bowed down to me." So

2

he told it to his father and his brothers; and his father rebuked him and said to him, "What is this dream that you have dreamed? Shall your mother and I and your brothers indeed come to bow down to the earth before you?" And his brothers envied him, but his father kept the matter in mind.

Genesis 37:9–11

By now, it has been recorded three times that Joseph's brothers hated him, and each time the dreaming only made it worse. Now their hatred had turned to envy.

What should Joseph do? Should he give up his dreams and live as his brothers were living? Oh, please, no. Giving up a dream is like death itself. You might as well be dead as dreamless. When God places a dream, any dream, in your spirit, you need to go after it with a passion. If not, you will never be completely fulfilled in this life.

Dreams do come true. Although Joseph was just a teenager when he had this particular dream, and it didn't come to pass until he was thirty years old (see Genesis 41:46), it did come to pass. In the meantime, there was a learning process that God was taking him through.

There is usually a period of time—and in Joseph's case, a considerable period of time—between the dreaming of the dream and the manifestation of what has been dreamed. So, just because your dream has not yet come to pass, don't give up on it. Your day is coming. And when it does, everything will change.

When Joseph dreamed his dream, his brothers laughed at him, but when it came to pass, they looked up to him. In Genesis 37 they hated him, but by Genesis 47 they had come to respect him. This is exactly what God wants to do for you.

The fact that the fulfillment of dreams takes time should not stop you. Go after your dream.

There are several important preliminary observations to be made about Joseph's dream. To begin with, it was unique. He dreamed that one day all of his family would be serving him. Most of us would not have that same dream, but God has a unique dream waiting for us too. Dare to be a dreamer.

Dare to Dream

Don't ever be afraid to dream, and don't ever be afraid to be a dreamer. I'm not just talking about dreams that come while you're asleep. Sometimes your dream can come to you while you're working on your job. It can come to you while you're standing at a bus stop. Very often dreams come to us while we're in church or in prayer at home, for God is the Author of great dreams.

We could compare the dreams God gives us to the previews of coming attractions we sometimes see with movies or television. Through a dream, He is giving us a peek into the future, and what we see is glorious. Never be afraid to dream.

Some are afraid to dream or to talk about their dreams because there are always those who make fun of dreams. But these mockers are wrong. Dreams are wonderful, so don't ever be afraid to dream and don't ever be afraid to dream large. It's not a shame for you not to reach your every goal, but it *is* a shame for you not to have any goals in the first place. The disgraceful thing is not failing to always reach your dream or see it manifested; the disgraceful thing is not to dream at all.

It's only lazy people who can't dream. Every one of us, young and old alike, should have a dream and be trusting the Lord for something bigger and better. It's a sin not to want to live the life God has destined us for.

If someone would ask you today, "Where are you headed in the next ten years?" or "What are you working toward over the next five years?" would you have an answer? I would be ashamed to say no, and I hope you would too.

Every person alive should have goals—short-term goals, mid-range goals, and long-term goals. After all, we have to be working toward something. If not, our lives have very little meaning.

Next year, five years from now, or ten years from now, what do you hope to have accomplished for your family? For your career? For your economic future? What are you doing to cause your unique talents to be put to use? Our Lord said to His church,

See, I have set before you an open door, and no one can shut it.
Revelation 3:8

This is the promise, but are you traveling down the corridors of obedience? What are you doing to make your dreams come to pass? You can't just sleep late every morning and never leave the house and expect your life to change for the better. If you want to get what you've never had, you must be willing to do what you've never done.

As we have already seen, the dreams were not the only reason Joseph's brothers hated him. Although he could do nothing about their attitude, his biggest mistake was probably telling them about the dreams at all. Sometimes we just need to keep our dreams to ourselves. By telling them, Joseph only intensified their hated of him. Those who refuse to dream cannot understand those who do.

Another reason you can't share your dream with just anyone is that there are many dream-killers out there. They don't want to see your dream come true, so they'll do everything they can to discourage you and keep you from it. It would be well for us to remember the wise words of Solomon:

A fool vents all his feelings, but a wise man holds them back.
Proverbs 29:11

There are things that God will tell you that are not for everyone else to know. Sometimes you just have to hold them in. Later, when events unfold, everyone else is surprised, but God has already shown you what will transpire.

Having a dream will keep you focused on the Lord. When you need Him to do something for you, it places you in a position of trust and dependence upon Him. This is healthy. I never want to be totally free of need in my own life.

As long as I have needs, God has a job, for He supplies all of my needs. I don't ever want Him to be unemployed in that regard. Still, there are many adults who have no dreams at all. They have never even considered what they are working toward.

So it's good to dream, and when you begin to dream, others may become jealous and angry. And if they're jealous now just because you're dreaming it, how will it be when you actually start living it? They hated Joseph, and some will hate you too.

We can deduce something from this fact. The fact that Joseph's brothers were angry with him for having a dream shows us that they didn't have one themselves. Visionaries are never intimidated by others who have great visions, and dreamers are perfectly comfortable around other dreamers. The only people who have a problem with dreamers are those who are bankrupt of dreams themselves.

When I see a brother's dream beginning to unfold, it doesn't make me angry. To the contrary, I'm excited for him—and not only for him, but for myself as well. I also have a dream, and if my brother's dream is coming true, then I know that it's only a matter of time before mine will too. My dream is different from his dream, but the same God who gave him his dream gave me mine too. And if God helps him to see his dream come true, how could He do any less for me?

In time, the hatred of Joseph's brothers reached it peak, and they sought a way to do him harm:

> *Now when they saw him afar off, even before he came near them, they conspired against him to kill him. Then they said to one another, "Look, this dreamer is coming! Come therefore, let us now kill him and cast him into some pit; and we shall say, 'Some wild beast has devoured him.' We shall see what will become of his dreams!"*
>
> Genesis 37:18–20

Joseph was saved from this threat only because one of his older brothers, Reuben, took pity on him:

> *But Reuben heard it, and he delivered him out of their hands, and said, "Let us not kill him." And Reuben said to them, "Shed no blood, but cast him into this pit which is in the wilderness, and do not lay a hand on him"—that he might deliver him out of their hands, and bring him back to his father.*
>
> Genesis 37:21–22

Unlike the other brothers, Reuben wasn't sure that he wanted to see Joseph die, but he did want to make him suffer a little:

> *So it came to pass, when Joseph had come to his brothers, that they stripped Joseph of his tunic, the tunic of many colors that was on him. Then they took him and cast him into a pit. And the pit was empty; there was no water in it.*
>
> Genesis 37:23–24

LIVING THE DREAM

On your way to fulfilling your dream, once in a while you might find yourself in some pit. You will undoubtedly encounter adversity and some detours, and there will be stumbling blocks along the way. But Joseph didn't allow the pit to overshadow his dream, and you can't either. This was just part of his preparation for the palace.

What might your pit be? It might be that moment when you're down and out, and you feel like saying, "What's the use?" The absolute wrong thing to do in that moment is to commence the "whys?"

This is what most Christians do. "Why is this happening to me?" "Why do people treat me like this?" "Why did God permit this, if He loves me?" Leave the "whys?" with God. Just trust Him. He knows what He's doing. It's all part of the process.

When Joseph found himself in the pit, he did some thinking. And his conclusion was that if he never got out of the pit alive, his dream obviously could not be fulfilled. And, since he knew that the dream was from God, and he knew that God could not lie, this meant that he *would* have to get out of the pit. If he didn't, then God was a liar, and that couldn't be the case.

So, even in the pit, Joseph didn't give in to pity. He knew that he would come out of there. God had shown him that his family would one day serve him, and they couldn't very well do that with him in the pit.

You may be down and out, but this fight is not over because what God has shown you has not yet been totally fulfilled. If you know that God has shown it to you, all you have to do is survive the pit. Say to yourself, "I'm here right now, but it won't always be like this. *I will* be coming out of this pit."

8

Oh, friend, you're on your way out now. Things may be looking bad at the moment, but don't give up on God. If He said it, He'll do it. If He spoke it, He'll bring it to pass.

Some may be causing a delay in the fulfillment of their own dreams because they really don't believe what God has shown them. If we really believe Him, we will thank Him for it every day until we see it with our eyes. We must keep the dream before us and praise Him as if it has already come to pass—and it will.

Friend, do you have a dream? Then go for it. Whatever the devil brings against you, don't let it stop your dream. Until the dream is fulfilled, you can know that God will bring you out of any trouble you experience in the process.

There are many fans of the late great NASCAR racer Dale Earnhardt. I had never been a stock car racing fan, but one day several years ago, I didn't have anything else to do on a Saturday, so I watched the famous Indy 500. I kept hearing that Dale Earnhardt was leading the race. Then, suddenly, he pulled off the track to make a pit stop.

That didn't make sense to me. If the object of the race was to get around the track five hundred times, why wouldn't he just keep on driving—especially when he was ahead? What I didn't know then was that the drivers had to change tires, refuel, and make some quick adjustments to their vehicles. So making a pit stop was not a tactical mistake, as I had first imagined, but rather a very wise move.

Then I realized what God was trying to show me in all of this. When the Lord has us in the pit, He's trying to make an attitude adjustment in us. He's trying to refuel us and get us ready for some serious racing. We *can* still win the race.

In that pit, Joseph didn't have anything else to do but call on God, and that's the very best kind of refueling we could do.

LIVING THE DREAM

Some of you may think that you've been in the pit much too long, but trust God that His promise is true. He said,

*And we know that **all things** work together for good to those who love God, to those who are the called according to His purpose.*

Romans 8:28

If the Lord keeps you in the pit for a day, a week, a month, or a year, trust His wisdom and take advantage of your time there to get ready for the greater things ahead. It's all part of the process.

When you have dared to dream, you must stand on the promise God has given you through your dream—no matter how impossible it looks. If your dream seems too big and too grand and too humanly impossible, that's good. Then you will not be able to do anything *but* trust God and depend on Him. And if you experience a setback somewhere along the way, let that be a setup for your comeback.

Just be sure you stay in the race, and never be afraid to dream.

Dare to Be Different

If you expect your dream to come true, you must dare to be different. You were not called to be just like someone else. God called you to be you.

You don't need to be in the club. You don't need to be part of the clique. You don't need to be invited to join the group. You can stand by yourself.

Joseph was not afraid to stand alone. God had shown him a dream, and he would follow it—whatever others did. In the dream, he had seen his family members bowing to him. It hadn't happened yet, but if God said it would, then it would.

Learning to Go After Your Dream

Joseph did come out of the pit—as he knew he would—but then he was thrust into another bad situation. Sold into slavery, he was taken to Egypt, and there he was sold to a man named Potiphar. Let us now skip to a later portion of the Bible narrative:

Now Joseph had been taken down to Egypt. And Potiphar, an officer of Pharaoh, captain of the guard, an Egyptian, bought him from the Ishmaelites who had taken him down there.

Genesis 39:1

Joseph had survived the pit because the Lord was with him, and now he surely knew that he could survive anything. His trip to Egypt must have been a nightmare, and he couldn't know what would become of him, but he knew that the Lord was with him.

That's the important thing. I don't mind any pit—as long as the Lord is there with me. The presence of the Lord with Joseph made him *"a successful man"* even in his dire circumstances:

The Lord was with Joseph, and he was a successful man; and he was in the house of his master the Egyptian.

Genesis 39:2

This is important. Joseph was *"successful,"* but he still had not obtained his dream. He was already *"successful,"* and he could have lived the rest of his life and died in that state. But what kept Joseph pressing forward was the fact that although he had become successful, he still had an unfulfilled dream.

Potiphar couldn't help but notice Joseph's good work:

And his master saw that the Lord was with him and that the Lord made all he did to prosper in his hand.

Genesis 39:3

11

This is wonderful. Can your co-workers see that the Lord is with you?

How did Potiphar and others see that the Lord was with Joseph? Could it have been in his positive attitude in the midst of adversity? Could it have been the serene look on his countenance in the presence of conflict? Could it have been that he maintained the right demeanor even in the midst of difficulty? Whatever it was, they saw that the Lord was with him. And, through this, God gave Joseph additional favor:

> *So Joseph found favor in his sight, and served him. Then he made him overseer of his house, and all that he had he put under his authority. So it was, from the time that he had made him overseer of his house and all that he had, that the LORD blessed the Egyptian's house for Joseph's sake; and the blessing of the LORD was on all that he had in the house and in the field.*
>
> Genesis 39:4–5

Now both Potiphar's house and fields were blessed just because Joseph was there. Why? Because God's favor was upon Joseph, and when His favor is upon you, you bless other people just by being in their presence.

Potiphar, seeing what was happening to everything under Joseph's control, then gave him even more authority:

> *Thus he left all that he had in Joseph's hand, and he did not know what he had except for the bread which he ate.*
>
> Genesis 39:6

In a relatively short period of time, Joseph came out of the pit and then was recognized as a prosperous and successful man. He was deemed so trustworthy that Potiphar left everything in his hands and didn't give anything a second thought. He knew that Joseph would take good care of it.

You can be sure that the devil was not happy with all of this, and he was about to make his move.

There was an interesting phrase attached to the end of this verse 6. It said,

> *Now Joseph was handsome in form and appearance.*
>
> Genesis 39:6

He was still young, he had a good body, and he was handsome. I'm a little jealous. But this youth and good build and handsomeness was about to subject Joseph to some special temptations:

> *And it came to pass after these things that his master's wife cast longing eyes on Joseph, and she said, "Lie with me."*
>
> Genesis 39:7

Isn't that just like the devil? Joseph was doing so well, and now this had to happen.

But I understand where Potiphar's wife was coming from. This young man was anointed. God's presence was on him. The favor of the Lord was upon him. And, on top of that, he was good-looking. He was well built. So, being the normal, healthy woman that she was, she began to lust after him.

As Potiphar's wife, she had a certain hold over Joseph, a certain authority, and she used it now to pressure him to lie with her. In the jargon of our day, she was saying: "Let's do the wild thing! Let's hook up; let's take it to the next level."

How could Joseph refuse? After all, this woman was the lady of the house. But, thank God, he did refuse:

But he refused and said to his master's wife, "Look, my master does not know what is with me in the house, and he has committed all that he has to my hand. There is no one greater in this house than I, nor has he kept back anything from me but you, because you are his wife. How then can I do this great wickedness, and sin against God?"

Genesis 39:8–9

Joseph was daring to be different. He called for a pause so that this woman could cool off. Didn't she understand that God had raised him up in the house and that he could have anything that he wanted—aside from her? Did she think that he would lay all of that aside for a few moments of stolen pleasure? Well, some might have done it, but not Joseph. He had a dream, and he was determined to see his dream come true. He could not allow anything to sidetrack him.

Some have suggested that it was customary in that time for Egyptian men to share their wives, so maybe what this woman was suggesting was not so out of the ordinary. And, if that was so, it would have been a convenient excuse to do what she was suggesting. But this was clearly not for Joseph. He was different. She had the wrong man. She may have hooked up with other servants, but not this one.

Why was Joseph so firm about this? Because what God had shown him was greater than any one-night stand. We have to dare to be different and stop living like we need people to affirm us at every point. If we don't know who we are, people will tell us. But we're not what they suggest. We're only what we answer to. They can call us whatever they want, but we don't have to answer. It's time to be different, and being different is what kept Joseph in the anointed life.

Learning to Go After Your Dream

Being different means that you sometimes have to stand by yourself. This was nothing new for Joseph. He had been in the pit, he had been sold into slavery in Egypt, and now he had been tempted by a beautiful and powerful woman, but through it all, he had maintained his dream. Having a dream will keep you focused and keep you from straying. Now, however, Joseph was about to face the most difficult part of his period of preparation for the palace.

When Joseph refused to give in to the desires of Potiphar's wife, she accused him of trying to rape her. Taking his coat, she set him up, and then she lied about him. That led to him being falsely imprisoned. What a terrible turn of events! One moment he was in charge of everything in a rich man's estate, and the next moment he was on his way to prison.

Some may find it strange that Joseph was not afraid. Most of us would have been terrified. But Joseph hadn't done anything wrong, and he knew that the Lord was still with him. If he could just remain faithful to God for a little while longer, he would soon begin to make a difference in the lives of many.

Dare to Make a Difference in the Lives of Others

It's time for each of us to make an impact on our world. It's time for you to make a difference where you work and where you live. Can you do that when people mistreat you? Yes, you can.

Joseph was now in prison, falsely accused. That does happen from time to time. Sometimes people will do things to hurt you—when you have done nothing but good to them. Leave it with the Lord and move on. It's all part of the process.

As Joseph was being marched to the prison in handcuffs, some may have been laughing and mocking him. Here was that high and mighty Hebrew at last getting his just desserts. He had fooled

15

everyone, making them believe that he was a righteous man, when all the time he had been a rapist. How terrible! What a deceiver!

But Joseph's only wrong had been to dare to dream. Now, in the prison, he continued to maintain his faith in God and to stay strong and sharp spiritually, believing that one day his opportunity would come. And, of course, it did:

> Then the butler and the baker of the king of Egypt, who were confined in the prison, dreamed a dream, both of them, each man's dream in one night and each man's dream with its own interpretation. And Joseph came in to them in the morning and looked at them, and saw that they were sad. So he asked Pharaoh's officers who were with him in the custody of his lord's house, saying, "Why do you look so sad today?" And they said to him, "We each have had a dream, and there is no interpreter of it." So Joseph said to them, "Do not interpretations belong to God? Tell them to me, please."
>
> Genesis 40:5–8

How confident Joseph was! He had obviously not allowed his wrongful imprisonment to cause his spirit to be bitter, and he knew that God was still with him.

The chief butler told his dream to Joseph first:

> Behold, in my dream a vine was before me, and in the vine were three branches; it was as though it budded, its blossoms shot forth, and it clusters brought forth ripe grapes. Then Pharaoh's cup was in my hand; and I took the grapes and pressed them into Pharaoh's cup, and placed the cup in Pharaoh's hand.
>
> Genesis 40:9–11

Learning to Go After Your Dream

Despite the fact that he had suffered so many wrongs and was even now imprisoned on false charges, Joseph immediately sensed the interpretation of the dream:

And Joseph said to him, "This is the interpretation of it: The three branches are three days. Now within three days Pharaoh will lift up your head and restore you to your place, and you will put Pharaoh's cup in his hand according to the former manner, when you were his butler."

Genesis 40:12–13

As Joseph was giving this interpretation to the chief butler, a thought was coming to him. If he was able to help this man, surely the man should be grateful enough to help him in return. He would ask the butler to remember him before Pharaoh once the servant was released and restored. And the man would be released and restored, for that was what God had shown him. Sure that the man would help him, Joseph took time to explain to him just who he was and how he had been unjustly imprisoned.

Well, sure enough, the chief butler was released and restored to his honored position. But when the time came, he was so relieved for his own skin that he didn't remember Joseph and neither did he mention his cause before Pharaoh, as he had promised in the prison he would.

This must have been very sad for Joseph. The word he had given to the man had been powerful and sharp in every detail. It was obviously the divine interpretation of the strange dream. In just three days, he had foreseen in the spirit, the man would be released from prison and restored to his position. Everything that had been taken from him would be restored. Now, it had all come to pass, in every detail, but the man was so caught up in the joy of the moment that he had forgotten the humble Hebrew who gave him the interpretation and helped to spare his life.

LIVING THE DREAM

This same thing may well happen to you, but don't worry about it. Whatever you make happen for someone else, God will make happen for you too. Years ago, people laughed at me for serving our former pastor. They called me his "flunky," and his "go-for." When I went into the barbershop or other public places, I was ridiculed, persecuted, and scorned. But ever since I became pastor of the church myself, the people who laughed at me are no longer laughing. Don't worry about what people do.

The Lord had helped Joseph to survive the pit, to survive slavery, to survive the lie against him and the false imprisonment, and now He helped him to survive the failures of men to fulfill their promises. And he continued to prepare for the palace.

For many of us, our dreams have not yet come to pass, and it looks like they never will, because we've been in the pit or the prison too long. This is surely because we haven't been taught how to prepare for the palace.

While you're in the pit or the prison, you need to praise God like you're already in the palace. Praise Him as if it's already done.

And as you praise God, think about your dream. See yourself in the palace and see yourself doing what God has called you to do. Never mind if the person next to you doesn't see the same vision or experience the same thing. That's okay. Your vision is unique.

Begin to praise God for being debt-free. Praise Him for the spouse He's going to give you. Praise Him for His provision for your life. Praise Him for a job or a better job. Praise Him for better benefits. Praise Him for a new house. Praise Him for a new car. Praise Him for the fulfillment of all of your dreams.

The dreams you dare to dream will surely come to pass, for all the forces of hell cannot stop them. The hatred of your brothers cannot stop them. Lies cannot stop them. The failure of your friends cannot stop them. The only thing that can stop them is if you give up on them. So never give up on your dream. Go for it. Give your dream a chance to come to pass.

Let God do it for you. Let Him open every door. Never stop trusting Him. Keep on believing. You may be in the pit right now or you may be in the prison, but it's not over yet. Start practicing your performance for the palace. You know what God has said, and if He said it, He will bring it to pass.

Learn to go after the promise God has given you, and before long you will find yourself *Living the Dream.*

LIVING THE DREAM

Chapter Two

LEARNING TO CONSIDER YOUR CALLING— WHEN NO ONE ELSE DOES

And Samuel said to Jesse, "Are all the young men here?" Then he said, "There remains yet the youngest, and there he is, keeping the sheep." And Samuel said to Jesse, "Send and bring him. For we will not sit down till he comes here." So he sent and brought him in. Now he was ruddy, with bright eyes, and good-looking. And the LORD said, "Arise, anoint him; for this is the one!" Then Samuel took the horn of oil and anointed him in the midst of his brothers; and the Spirit of the LORD came upon David from that day forward.
1 Samuel 16:11–13

You've been chosen. You may not have been considered by others, but you've been chosen nevertheless. Let me tell you what I mean by that.

Here in the first of Samuel's books, we have a wonderful image of an individual who has discovered his destiny in God. When people don't know their purpose in life and don't know their Creator, they have a tendency to live like animals. The one thing that intimidates the enemy more than anything else is when you begin to ask questions about your destiny, when you begin to seek and search out God's truths on this subject.

You might ask, "God, why am I here? Why was I created in the first place?" When this happens, the enemy knows that you're on the road to discovering your destiny, and he trembles.

Discover Rather Than Decide Your Destiny

Far too many members of the body of Christ are frustrated because they have decided their own destiny rather than discover their divine destiny. It's dangerous to stand back and see what someone is doing and then say, "You know, I think that's what I want to do too." It's dangerous to see what someone else has and then to say, "You know, I think it would be good if I had that too." This is no way to arrive at your destiny.

Ask the Spirit of God to enlighten you as to why you have been through the things you've been through. If you will listen to the Spirit, you will learn that it is so that you could be right where you are today.

The fact that the average person fails to discover any purpose in life explains a lot about our world and about why so many people don't like themselves. They don't like themselves because they don't know who they are. And, because they don't like themselves, they don't like any of the people around them either. As a result, there are a lot of angry people in our world today.

If you want some young man or woman to fall in love with you, first you have to love yourself. You must be able to look at yourself in the mirror and thank God for what you see. Make up your mind that you don't have to change yourself in order to find a suitable mate. The mate God has chosen for you will like you just as you are. Say, "I'm going to be just who God has called me to be, and I'm not going to lower my standards to try to get some-body's approval. I'm going to be me."

The Bible says, in Psalm 139:14, that we are *"fearfully and won-derfully made."* You're a masterpiece, and you must not desire to be like anyone else. Be content to be you, for no one can be you better than you can. That's one game that no one can beat you at. If other people have a problem with you being yourself, that's not your problem; it's their problem.

As a nation, we're spending billions of dollars every year on cosmetics and cosmetic surgery, and many spend a great deal of their time trying to find someone who will validate, or appreciate, them as a person. Our generation seems to be compliment hungry. Well, start complimenting yourself. Tell yourself everything that God has said about you. He made you the way you are for a purpose.

I'm not saying that we shouldn't comb our hair and put on makeup and some of the other things we do to improve our looks. That's fine. What I'm saying is that each of us has to learn to like himself. Once you accomplish that, then you can begin to like the people around you more.

If you can discover who you are and discover what God says about you and believe it more than you believe what society says, it will change your life. When you begin to believe what God says more than you believe what your parents and other relatives say, it will change you. When you begin to believe what God says more than you believe government agents or philosophers or counselors, it will change your life. Then, and only then, can you rise to your full potential and experience your God-given destiny.

The only reason your life has taken the unique twists and turns it has is that you have been chosen. You may not have been considered, but you've been chosen.

God said, "You're the one whom I'm going to bless and raise up." Do you think that the devil would have been attacking you the way he has if you were a nobody? The devil knows what's on the inside of you, and he's intimidated because you're about to step out and become who God knows you to be.

Believe what God says about you, and stop worrying about what man says. God says that you're *"the head and not the tail,"* *"above...and not beneath"* (Deuteronomy 28:13).

Everyone Is Anointed for Something

It's my personal conviction that every person alive is anointed to do something. God would not cause you to be born and not give you a special anointing. You may not have discovered it yet, but you are anointed for something.

The only reason you haven't lost you mind, with all the torment you've been going through over the last few years, is that the devil can't penetrate the anointing, and you're anointed.

This word *anoint* and the accompanying words, *anointing* and *anointed*, are very loosely used these days. But let me tell you what happens when an individual is anointed. Being anointed means that you are empowered and set apart for a particular task, a particular service. To be anointed means to be empowered; it means to be enabled; it means to be equipped in the service of God. And that means that you have everything you need to get the job done.

Your unique anointing means that God has put something on you that He has not put on your neighbor. You particular anointing will bring God glory.

The anointing upon a person's life is not just for preaching. It's not just for shouting. It's not just for prophesying. No! The anointing is for service.

When you realize that you are anointed and that your anointing is unique, it will change the way you think about yourself. And when you think differently about yourself, you will no longer be moved by what others say. It will go right over your head.

David's anointing came about through King Saul's failure. God had anointed Saul to be king, but when He told Saul to destroy the Amalekites and not to save anyone or anything among them, he disobeyed. The people and their beasts must all be killed, God said, but Saul did not see the reasonableness of this, and he did as many of us do: He decided to modify the instructions of the Lord. God had said, "Kill everything," but Saul only gave Him partial obedience.

When this happened, God fired Saul from his position. He rejected him as king. He might still have sat on his throne, but he no longer enjoyed God's blessings.

Now Israel needed another king. So God immediately called Samuel, His prophet, and told him to go to the house of one Jesse in Bethlehem. There, among this man's sons, he would find and anoint a replacement for King Saul.

Samuel was worried that if Saul heard about this trip, he might have him killed. The Lord told him to take a heifer with him and to say that he was going to sacrifice to the Lord.

Samuel went to Jesse's house because someone there was predestined to become a king. In this big word *predestination*, the prefix *pre* means "before." Predestination represents our completed end even before we get started. *"Pre,"* or before…that's the way our destiny is decided. You were predestined before you even got here.

God told Jeremiah,

Before I formed you in the womb I knew you; before you were born I sanctified you; I ordained you a prophet to the nations.
                                                                    Jeremiah 1:5

God first sees the end of a thing, and then He backs up and works at it from the other end. That's what predestination is all about, and you are predestined for greatness.

It had not been easy for Samuel to accept the fact that Saul had failed, since he had been called upon to anoint Saul as king also. But Saul had his chance at greatness, and he had "blown it," as we say.

Now the LORD said to Samuel, "How long will you mourn for Saul, seeing I have rejected him from reigning over Israel? Fill your horn with oil, and go; I am sending you to Jesse the Bethlehemite. For I have provided Myself a king among his sons."
                                                                    1 Samuel 16:1

In a very real sense, the Lord had said to Samuel, "Stop crying. It's over." And when God says it's over, it's over, and we need to move on.

God Doesn't Choose as Men Do

It was then that Samuel had been sent to the house of Jesse, and he was told to take his horn of anointing oil with him. God had someone in mind for this very special and demanding position.

It's interesting that God said to Samuel that He was providing *Himself* with a king. So David would be the Lord's king, not the people's king. And this new king was to be found among the sons of Jesse. That much Samuel knew.

But how should Samuel go about this all-important task of choosing a new king? God showed him exactly how to proceed:

Then invite Jesse to the sacrifice, and I will show you what you shall do; you shall anoint for Me the one I name to you.

1 Samuel 16:3

That sounded easy enough. God would show His prophet which son to anoint.

Well, we all know the story. All of the sons of Jesse, one by one, passed before Samuel, from the oldest to the youngest, and each time Samuel (and Jesse) thought they had found the right one for the job. It started with Eliab:

So it was, when they came, that he looked at Eliab and said, "Surely the LORD's anointed is before Him!"

1 Samuel 16:6

Eliab was tall and broad-shouldered, and he would have looked very good sitting on the throne of Israel. Saul was a tall man himself, and, because he had been the first king, everyone now believed that the king should be tall, head and shoulders above everyone else.

When Eliab entered the room, Samuel thought to himself, *This isn't going to be as hard a job as I thought. That's him right there. Look at those broad shoulders. Look at that great stride. Look at the way he carries himself. Eliab will represent Israel well.*

But God didn't see it the way Samuel did:

But the LORD said to Samuel, "Do not look at his appearance or at his physical stature, because I have refused him. For the LORD does not see as man sees; for man looks at the outward appearance, but the LORD looks at the heart."

1 Samuel 16:7

What Samuel did was not surprising. We humans often make our choices based on the wrong set of criteria. That's how many of us get ourselves into so much trouble. We look at the external, and if we like what we see, we make a hasty decision to accept it. That's the way many young people get hooked up with a mate who's superficial and unspiritual.

God doesn't choose the way man does. He always looks on the heart. "No!" He said to Saumuel, "Eliab's not the one."

Wow! I wonder what Samuel was feeling about then. He must have been confused and troubled. Eliab had seemed so qualified, but if God had refused him, how could Samuel ever hope to find the right one?

They kept trying:

So Jesse called Abinadab, and made him pass before Samuel. And he said, "Neither has the LORD chosen this one." Then Jesse made Shammah pass by. And he said, "Neither has the LORD chosen this one." Thus Jesse made seven of his sons pass before Samuel. And Samuel said to Jesse, "The LORD has not chosen these."

1 Samuel 16:8–10

It seems obvious that Eliab had been his father's first choice, and when he failed the test, Jesse must have been surprised. Then he quickly recovered and said, "Well, now, if it's not Eliab, then it has to be Abinadab." And when Abinadab also was rejected, Jesse said, "Well, then, it has to be Shammah." But no again. Now he was on his fourth son, and then the fifth, the sixth, and the seventh.

By this time, Jesse was probably very confused and frustrated. He may have been thinking that Samuel had missed it this time. They had not found the promised king among all of his sons.

It was only then that this same thought dawned on Samuel and he asked, "Wait a minute. Are all of your sons here?"

Now Jesse didn't know what to say. No, not all of his sons were there present, but, yes, all of his sons who were being considered for the job were there. After all, they were talking about kingly material.

Well, for the sake of conversation, there was one more son, but no one would consider him. He was out doing what he did best: keeping his father's smelly sheep. He was not in contention for this position because he was too young and too inexperienced, and he seemed rather strange.

But Samuel insisted, "Send and bring him in here, because we can't sit down until he comes." So the banqueting came to a standstill, and they could go no further until David arrived.

David Hadn't Even Been Invited

This had been an extremely important occasion, and everyone was there. Jesse was there, Samuel was there, and Jesse's older sons were there, but others were there too. Samuel had invited all the elders of Bethlehem to witness this historic event. But David, God's guest of honor, was not there. No one had even considered him. Think about that. It had never even crossed their minds that David might be the one.

The preacher was ready, the father was ready, all the other brothers were ready, and the elders were ready, but somehow David had not been summoned. He was clearly the least among them. And if you are the least among your family, rejoice, because you're a prime candidate for God's anointing too.

If you did something in the past that you're ashamed of, if you have a lot of strikes against you, rejoice. You're a prime candidate for the anointing. You may be the one whom God will use.

David's brothers had their own unique anointing, but it was not an anointing to be king. They were anointed to do something, but that something was not to sit on the throne of Israel. The kingly anointing had been reserved for someone whom they had not considered to be a worthy candidate.

Suddenly they were having a discussion about David, and he wasn't even around. He didn't have a clue that he was about to be pushed onto God's stage, that he was about to enter into his God-given destiny. And you may not know it either, but you're on people's minds. They're talking about you too. While you're not around, God is working on your behalf.

I hope you have enough sense to know that what's yours is yours. Don't just sit there. Claim it. If God says it's yours, then it's yours. So take it.

David was shut out, and some of you know what that feels like. You surely may have felt rejection at some point in your life. You may know what it's like to be knocked down, stepped on, and walked over. But that's okay. Your day is coming. Get ready for the palace.

It may seem that everyone else has had their turn but you, but don't worry. Your turn is coming. Wait patiently, and prepare as you wait.

I don't care how old you are, I don't care how young you are, and I don't even care how many times you've been married. It's your turn. The devil should have killed you when he had the chance because you're about to rise as an anointed one.

Learning to Consider Your Calling—When No One Else Does

Anointed in the Presence of Your Detractors

David finally came. He was still in his sheep-keeping clothes, and he still smelled like the field. Still, he was, according to the Bible, a good-looking boy:

> *Now he was ruddy, with bright eyes, and good-looking.*
>
> 1 Samuel 16:12

I can somehow picture David as he entered the room. "Yes?" he said. "Did someone call me?" And, as he entered, he did it in his unassuming way. He was the most insignificant member of the family, one who had been chosen without ever having been considered.

In that moment, God spoke to Samuel:

> *"Arise, anoint him; for this is the one!"*
>
> 1 Samuel 16:12

What a glorious moment that was! David must have been overwhelmed with gratitude. His long search for God had paid off. His faithfulness to the One he loved so much would now be evident to all.

And I want to tell you today that you're the one God is looking for too. He has a special job for you to perform. That's why the devil has been attacking you. You're God's choice.

What an exciting moment! Samuel raised the horn of oil over David:

> *Then Samuel took the horn of oil and anointed him in the midst of his brothers; and the Spirit of the LORD came upon David from that day forward.*
>
> 1 Samuel 16:13

Notice how God did it. He purposely honored David in the presence of those who had discounted him. They had shut him out, but God raised him up. They didn't even consider him, but God chose him anyway.

Later, David would sing,

You prepare a table before me in the presence of my enemies.
Psalm 23:5

Many don't yet know what you are made of, but in time, they will. Your time to shine is coming.

Can you imagine how those brothers reacted when they saw the anointing come upon their youngest brother? Surely they were jealous because David now had something they didn't have. Now they knew that David, whom they had long considered to be ordinary, was really extraordinary.

God is saying the same thing about you. He knows how to take an ordinary person and give him or her something extra. That makes any man or woman extraordinary.

God has made many of you who were ordinary into extraordinary individuals, but it's possible that you haven't yet discovered what that something extra you have is. You may sense that you have it. You may realize that there's something different about you that doesn't allow you to fit in with all the rest of the crowd. But soon your time will come, and you'll see more fully what God has done for you that is unique and special.

David Disappeared Again

It had taken the prophet a long time to get around to David. Samuel had arrived in Bethlehem in verse 4, but then verses 5 though 11 had gone by, and the lad was nowhere to be seen.

Finally, he had arrived and been anointed. Now, again, after his anointing, a similar thing happened. He was anointed in verse 13, and then he was not heard from again for many verses. The narrative goes back to Saul, who was still sitting on the throne.

Where was David? He was anointed, but he had disappeared— at least for the time being. He had been predestined, and he now knew that he would one day rule all Israel, but, for the moment, he had gone back to his sheepfold, back to his preparation for the palace. He would eventually live the dream, but in the meantime, he must prepare more for it.

David must have felt very differently now. He was a kid with a king's anointing, and it must have been hard for him to concentrate on his work. He had been anointed to rule, not to mess with dirty sheep. But David was patient and wise, and he went back to practicing for the palace.

You, too, know that there is more to your anointing than your environment would indicate. Your co-workers may retire from that position, but you're there for an entirely different purpose. Your anointing will take you much higher.

David wasn't heard of again until verse 18. Then there was a need for an anointed person to do a very special task. An evil spirit had come upon Saul, and someone was needed who could drive it away. It was then that someone thought of David and said, "Wait a minute, I know someone who fits the bill perfectly."

David was out of sight, but people in high places were talking about him again, and they're talking about you too. Sometimes people talk about you, and what they say is not good. But be glad when people who don't even know you are suddenly talking about you. Even negative publicity is better than no publicity at all.

This was a very confusing time for David. The anointing was upon him, and he knew he had it. Still, Saul remained in the office of king. David had the power, but Saul still had the position. I don't know about you, but I'd much rather have the power than the position.

Many feel just the opposite, and that's okay. They can have the position every time. Give me the power.

Pharaoh, for instance, had the position, but Moses had the power. Nebuchadnezzar had the position, but Daniel had the power. Ahab had the position, but Elijah had the power. Herod had the position, but Jesus had the power. For the foreseeable future, Saul held the position, but that would change in time. It always does when we're faithful and patient.

Some of you have been anointed, but you still have to ride the bus. You've been anointed, but you still live from paycheck to paycheck. You've been anointed, but you still don't have a husband. You've been anointed, but you're still in the developing stages. God wants to inform you that He's getting ready to move on your behalf. Your day is coming. You've been faithful, and now it will soon be your turn. It's about time to take your place in the palace.

David had been predestined for the palace from birth, but after predestination comes preparation, and only after preparation does promotion come. Eventually, David was summoned to the palace. This first trip, however, would be as a servant, not as king.

If you will learn to serve others, you can learn a lot from them. When you serve the king, you have the opportunity to see how a king lives and how you will live once you are king.

You can say to the devil, "Everything that I've been through is for a purpose. I had to go through all of that so I could be who I'm destined to be. And I may not be all that just yet, but I've been anointed, and I have the power. I just need to get ready to rule."

Not many thought I would be where I am today. When God moved me up to this position, they were amazed. To them, I seemed like a nobody coming out of nowhere. But I had been in preparation. Like David, I was hidden away while others took the limelight…until I was, at last, prepared.

And you, too, have been chosen—whether men considered you to be qualified or not. It doesn't matter if you're the least among your family and friends, if you have made a mess of your life in the past, if you've been married several times, had children out of wedlock, and done some other terrible things. God says, "Don't look at the appearance. I don't choose like that. I don't look at age. I don't look at stature. I don't look at human qualifications. I look at a person's heart."

You've been chosen. At times, it seemed like you would lose your mind. You have been misunderstood, ostracized, and criticized, but that doesn't change anything. You're chosen, and the devil knows it.

He has tried to make a mockery of your faith, trying his best to make you look bad. He loves to do that. But it won't work because you've been chosen. You have a great destiny in God.

Think about it. The day David was born he was destined to become the king of Israel. As he grew up, he was so short that everyone wondered if he would ever amount to much. Then, he was consigned to keeping a bunch of smelly sheep. But that didn't change anything. All the while, he was going through a preparation process, getting ready for the palace, getting ready to live his dream.

Many of us tend to fight the process. Stop fighting. Go through whatever you have to go through because what's yours is yours, and nothing can change it.

It may seem like you're losing a lot of time, but God will help you make up for lost time later on. You're about to get double for all your trouble. You're about to be rewarded for everything you've been through.

The Lord is about to raise you up. And, when He does it, it won't be done in a closet. He will do it in the sight of your brothers—those same ones who have lied about you and tried to kick you to the side. They can't prevent your rise because God Himself will raise you up. You have destiny and purpose, and you need to know who you are.

If you are faithful in the pasture, God will know that He can trust you in the palace. Get ready to begin *Living the Dream*.

Chapter Three

LEARNING TO MOVE FROM INSECURITY TO CONFIDENCE

So Israel was greatly impoverished because of the Midianites, and the children of Israel cried out to the LORD. And it came to pass, when the children of Israel cried out to the LORD because of the Midianites, that the LORD sent a prophet to the children of Israel, who said to them, "Thus says the LORD God of Israel: 'I brought you up from Egypt and brought you out of the house of bondage; and I delivered you out of the hand of the Egyptians and out of the hand of all who oppressed you, and drove them out before you and gave you their land. Also I said to you, "I am the LORD your God; do not fear the gods of the Amorites, in whose land you dwell. But you have not obeyed My voice." ' "

Judges 6:6–10

LIVING THE DREAM

The story of a third Bible character, a man named Gideon, is in many ways comparable to that of Joseph and David. When Gideon ruled Israel, there were no kings as yet. Instead, the people were ruled by anointed judges, set in place by God Himself. But Israel's judges were, in most every other way, comparable to the kings who followed them. God's judges did everything else that kings did. They just didn't wear a crown.

The last of the judges was Samuel, the man who set Saul in as king and then anointed his replacement David. Gideon had been judge during a previous generation. That he was a judge at all was a great miracle, and that is our focus in this chapter.

The context of the story I want to base this chapter on is a little lengthy, but it will be worth our forbearance:

> And the Angel of the Lord appeared to him [Gideon], and said to him, "The Lord is with you, you mighty man of valor!" And Gideon said to Him, "O my lord, if the Lord is with us, why then has all this happened to us? And where are all His miracles which our fathers told us about saying, 'Did not the Lord bring us up from Egypt?' But now the Lord has forsaken us and delivered us into the hands of the Midianites." Then the Lord turned to him and said, "Go in this might of yours, and you shall save Israel from the hand of the Midianites. Have I not sent you?" So he said to Him, "O my Lord, how can I save Israel? Indeed my clan is the weakest in Manasseh, and I am the least in my father's house." And the Lord said to him, "Surely I will be with you, and you shall defeat the Midianites as one man."
>
> Judges 6:12–16

Not one of us wants to go to heaven before experiencing our destinies here on Earth. And in order to discover your destiny, the first thing you must do is to break away from your insecurities

38

into a life of confidence. This means a radical change in your thinking.

The Bible says,

For as he thinks in his heart, so is he.

Proverbs 23:7

This being true, if the devil can keep you timid and afraid, if he can keep you locked in a cage of insecurity, then he knows that you will never tap into your God-given destiny and purpose.

I don't mean to be arrogant, but I know that I must be somebody, and no one can tell me that I'm a nobody. When I look back at the progression of my life, I can see that there was a purpose to it all. And if you don't think the same about yourself, you need to break out of your closet of insecurity and begin to live with confidence.

You should say, "Yes, I've made some mistakes in the past, but I can do all things through Christ who strengthens me. I may have some bumps and bruises, but I look like somebody to me. In fact, I look like a champion, like a warrior. I may have been to hell and back, but I still have my joy."

It's time for you to move into the realm of destiny, and when you do, the devil will be sorry he ever tried to hurt you. He thought he was discouraging you and dragging you down, but what he didn't know was that he was really helping you to discover who you were in the Lord.

As we have seen with Samuel, we humans are much too prone to judge people by their looks, what they have on, their outward appearance. And we've also heard things said about certain people, and consequently we treat them a certain way because of it. But what we heard might not be true at all. We may be judging them unfairly.

Sometimes we meet people and they don't like us even before they have a chance to get to know us. How can that be? It takes time to get to know someone.

But you know who you are, so forget about what other people think. It's time to break out of your cage of insecurity. When you enter a room, the atmosphere should change—because of who you are in Christ.

Your fellow employees may not realize that you're the one who is holding the company together. That's not an arrogant statement. It's walking with confidence.

I want you to begin to walk like the respected veteran of war that you are. I want you to be able to look at the devil and say, "Look out, devil. I'm up now, and I'm ready to face whatever I have to face and be victorious. You thought you had me yesterday, last week, and last month, but I'm still here. So, move out of my way."

Somehow you have to break away from your insecurities. Studies have proven that our thinking controls our behavior. Whatever you ponder will influence the way you act. If your mom or your dad told you that you were worthless and that you would never amount to anything, or if someone told you that you were an accident or that you were a misfit, you will live a limited life until that negative thought pattern is broken.

That's why God places people into our lives who can show us from His Word who we really are. We're not who people call us; we are who God says we are.

If, all of your life, you've been told that you're average, then you'll never have more than an average job and you'll never have more than an average life in every other way. You'll drive an average car and wear average clothes, and regardless of how you try to change yourself, you'll still look average. You'll go on in this average way until that negative thought pattern is broken.

Learning to Move from Insecurity to Confidence

If no one ever comes into your life to stimulate your spirit, if no one ever challenges you to believe for more and to reach for the stars, you'll never do it. You simply are a result of what has been spoken over your life—for good or for evil.

Gideon Was Barely Making It When God Called Him

Gideon was like many of us. When we first meet him, he's in a very sad state. He's poor, but he's worse than poor. The country in which he lives has been overrun by foreign marauders who stole everything they could get their hands on and drove the people of the land into hiding. These men were known as the Midianites.

In that moment, the last thing on Gideon's mind was his God-given destiny. He was scratching around just trying to get enough food together to stay alive. All he could think about was his next meal. In the opening scene, we see him hiding in a winepress, trying to gather a few grains of wheat for the next day.

Many of us can identify with this. We know what it is to not feel like we can make it through the day. But things can change—if Gideon can change his way of thinking.

He, like many of us, had developed a negative thought pattern, one that said, "This is the way life is, and this is the way it's going to be. I'll just go to work, pay bills, and have problems the rest of my life. Grandmother never had anything, Mama never had anything, and now it's my turn to have nothing. Anyway, I barely finished high school, and I dropped out of college. I have such a large student loan that it will take me forever to pay it off. I need a job, any job. It won't be high-paying, maybe just enough for me to get by on, but I'll have make it do."

And we often go through life just like that—willing to get by, living our average life, just being who we are and not daring to do anything different. This may be fine until we hear the Word of the Lord, but after that it will no longer do.

God has another plan for your life. He wants you to know that the devil is a liar. It may be true that your mama had nothing, but God wants to move you to another level. It's time to break the negative thought pattern that keeps you average!

All Gideon wanted to do was to stay alive, and his time was consumed with trying to eke out a living. Then something happened one day that changed everything. The angel of the Lord appeared to him and greeted him in a very strange way: *"The Lord is with you, you mighty man of valor!"*

Imagine that! This man was poor, he was a nobody, and he was insignificant, but still the Lord said to him that He was with him and that He saw him very differently than he saw himself. In God's eyes, Gideon was a *"mighty man of valor."*

That's exactly what God does. He calls us what we will be— even when we're not there yet and even when we don't know when we might get there.

I somehow imagine that Gideon kept right on working that day, sure that this man, whoever he was, could not be talking to him. "I'm just trying to make it. This man must be talking to someone else." It must have taken him a while to realize that he was the one being addressed.

And somehow I imagine that the very same thing has happened to you. God has been calling you, and you didn't even know it. He has been speaking some things to you, but you haven't even answered Him because you didn't realize that He was talking to you or that He could be talking to you.

The reason is that we don't recognize the title He places on us. *That's not me,* we think. We only see ourselves as we are now, but God sees us as we will be. He sees us according to His will to bless us in the future.

On September 27, 1966, in a hospital in Louisiana, God looked into a bassinet, and there He saw a little black baby boy who weighed seven pounds and twelve ounces. When God saw him, He said, "Look at that prophet. Look at that bishop. Look at that world leader." I was that little boy.

And when my mother was leaving the hospital a few days later, the Lord probably said to her, "Be careful with My prophet, and handle the man of God gently, because I have a great future for him.

"As he's growing up, make him go to church when he doesn't want to, and when he reaches adolescence, don't let him be like all the other young people, staying out all hours of the night. Maintain some rules over his life until I can get a hold on him and put him where he's supposed to be."

It took me a while to discover my destiny—just as it did Gideon—so I understand when you feel confused about your future too.

When the angel found Gideon that day, he didn't say anything negative to him at all. He didn't say, for instance, "My, what a terrible situation you're in!" or "My, how will you make it?" or "Boy, you certainly are struggling." He didn't say anything about how unfair life was or how everyone was having the same struggle.

Many of us are happy if we can just get to work on time and keep our heads above water. "Lord, just give me a little dwelling place here," we say, "and that will be enough for me. I don't need all the finer things of life. Just keep some shoes on my feet and some clothes on my back, and I'll be fine."

But God had other ideas for Gideon, and He has other ideas for you too. He knows that there's greatness on the inside of you. You have a destiny. You have no idea yet of how God will use you and bless you, and you're not moving forward because the labels that have been attached to your life have locked you into a certain mold. Well, it's time for some new labels.

Gideon was confused by the words of the angel. If God was with him, then why did everything seem to be going wrong? If God was with him, then why was he living from hand to mouth? If God was with him, why was he being oppressed by these wicked men?

We understand that reasoning. We often think, *If the Lord is with me, why am I on this dead-end job? If I'm so blessed, why am I struggling in this way just to exist?*

Gideon then reminded the angel that God had done miracles for previous generations, bringing them out of Egypt by many signs and wonders. But He seemingly hadn't been hearing the pleas for help from Gideon and his family. Where was God?

There was even a touch of bitterness in Gideon's words: *"But now the LORD has forsaken us and delivered us into the hands of the Midianites."* He had begun to talk back to the angel now.

In our modern way of expressing it, Gideon was saying, "Listen, I don't know who you are, but obviously you're not up on the latest. You're talking about the Lord being with me, so you must not understand what's going on here about now. Our entire nation has been overrun by the Midianites. And you see what I'm doing here? I'm just trying to gather enough wheat to take home to my family to make bread. We're desperate.

"You're talking about the Lord being with me... Well, where are all of His miracles? We could use a few right now."

But the answer from the angel was astonishing: *"Go in this might of yours, and you shall save Israel from the hand of the Midianites. Have I not sent you?"* (verse 14)

Learning to Move from Insecurity to Confidence

What was that? Here the man was barely existing, and God was going to use him to save Israel from the hands of the Midianites? This had to be a fantasy.

Again Gideon answered rather sarcastically, "Since you obviously don't know who I am, let me tell you. First of all, my family is the weakest in all Manasseh. And on top of that, I'm the least in my father's house. Maybe what you're saying could be believable—if my family had money or if my family had some better contacts. But in the family I grew up in, no one has ever done anything of importance. We're all struggling. No, I'm not from one of the more prestigious tribes. We're just poor farmers. And then you say that God is going to use me? Where did that come from?"

A Spark Was Beginning to Burn

But a spark was beginning to burn in Gideon's spirit. Could it be true? Could this be a real messenger from the Lord? He decided to test it.

"Okay, if I have indeed found favor in the Lord's sight, and you say that you're His angel, then show me a sign. Give me some proof. But, first, let me run and get an offering. Then I'll bring it back to you."

When Gideon had prepared his offering, the angel proceeded to give the desired sign:

Then the Angel of the LORD put out the end of the staff that was in His hand, and touched the meat and the unleavened bread; and the fire rose out of the rock and consumed the meat and the unleavened bread. And the Angel of the LORD departed out of his sight.

Judges 6:21

I love that about God. He's willing to meet us where we are. He had given Gideon the sign he desired. This changed Gideon's way of thinking dramatically:

Now Gideon perceived that He was the Angel of the LORD. So Gideon said, "Alas, O Lord GOD! For I have seen the Angel of the LORD face to face."

Judges 6:22

This word *perceived* means that he understood something in his spirit. He suddenly realized that this was the Angel of the Lord. Now everything that the angel had said began to make sense to him. But would he die because he had seen the Lord face to face?

Then the LORD said to him, "Peace be with you; do not fear, you shall not die."

Judges 6:23

"Gideon," the angel was saying, "don't worry about what's happening around you. You won't die because you have a purpose for living. I'm bound to preserve your life because before you were born, it was already determined that you would be the one chosen to deliver Israel from the Midianites.

"So what I need now, Gideon," I imagine the angel continuing, "is for you to go through the process so that you can stumble upon your destiny. You're about to find out why you were created."

Now Gideon was getting excited. Not only had the Lord spoken positively to him, but He also had reinforced His words with supernatural signs. Gideon was ready to believe:

So Gideon built an altar there to the LORD, and called it The-LORD-Is-Peace. To this day it is still in Ophrah of the Abriezites.

Judges 6:24

Learning to Move from Insecurity to Confidence

Gideon now knew that he was talking to Jehovah Shalom, so he built the altar and called it, "The Lord is Peace." The encounter with the Angel of the Lord had transformed his thinking.

Because of the impact of the angel's words on his mind, he suddenly began to look at the devastation around him through very different eyes. Now, everything that had irritated him in the past no longer did. Now it didn't faze him at all. The reason was that he could now see the larger picture.

That's what's happening to you right now. The people on your job can't understand why you haven't lost your mind, why you haven't had a nervous breakdown, why you're still going to church, still giving God the praise, when they know all that you've been through. But what they don't know is that you have begun to see the larger picture.

You know that God has left you here on earth for a reason. That's why the devil couldn't kill you in a car wreck, when you woke up as your vehicle was leaving the road. That's why God has preserved you through everything you've been through. And, ultimately, He has given you peace.

You may just now be discovering the fact that there's greatness on the inside of you. God is about to use you like you've never been used before. He's about to blow your world apart and put it back together again. He's about to do something very special in your life. In the natural you may not qualify, but in reality you're a prime candidate for God to use.

If you feel that you're too insignificant for God to use, you're just the one He can use. Yes, you—you, who had the abortion, you, who had babies out of wedlock, you, who are from the lowest part of town.

Yes, you may have made a mess of things, but you're still qualified. The worse your past is, the brighter your future is going to be. God can't use people who have never had a problem. He wants people who know that they need Him, people who know that they can't get the job done without His help.

He's calling you because destiny is upon you, greatness is on the inside of you, and it's time for you to break your insecurity and receive your confidence. Just go for it.

It doesn't matter how big the thing is that God speaks to you or how impossible it seems. It's yours. Just take it.

It's your turn. Others have received their blessings, and it's time for you to receive yours. Recognize that what's yours is yours, and nobody can stop you from receiving it.

Don't Hang Around with Insecure People

Surely Gideon must have been strongly influenced by the people around him. His negative attitude may well have been inherited from previous generations. Or it may have come from friends or family members.

Too many of us have developed friendships with insecure people, and when you're hanging around with insecure people, you're on dangerous ground. It's not good to be too close to people who don't know who they are and surely don't know who you really are. They will say anything at all about you or to you because insecure people feel like they have to tear someone else down so that they can build themselves up.

People rarely talk to us like the Angel of the Lord did to Gideon, so we need to purge ourselves of some of the negative influences in our lives and let God prove His power to us.

The things that God has promised you are in the making. You're almost there. You can stop having your little pity party and repent. Say to everyone around you, "I have decided to be who

God says I am. I've been trying to fit into the thought patterns of others, but now it's time to go God's way."

He was able to look at Gideon, who was broke and discouraged, and see something that Gideon's parents had not seen, his wife had not seen, and his friends had not seen. And with the new title He gave the man, came a new way of thinking and a totally new self-image. Before long, Gideon was ready to lead the nation to war against the Midianites.

It Was All Done Supernaturally

When the time came for Gideon to lead the armies of Israel out to battle, he had, rather amazingly, been able to gather more than twenty thousand men to fight. This was a great accomplishment. He was amazed, therefore, when God said to him, *"The people...are too many"* (Judges 7:2).

Gideon was perplexed. The enemies who had invaded the land seemed to be beyond numbering, and so he had been praying for more men to join him. Now God was telling him that he had too many. The Lord's concern was that if Gideon fought with so many men, he and the enemy as well would think that his victory had come at his own hand. This would not do, for although God intended to give Gideon the victory, He wanted all the glory. So He told Gideon to reduce his numbers.

Gideon cut his troops back to ten thousand and again prepared for battle, but God insisted that there were still too many. I learned a long time ago that God usually gives us maximum supplies with minimal support, and He does it so that He can receive all the glory.

Eventually Gideon's troops were cut all the way back to three hundred, and it was time to move out. God had called him a mighty man of valor when he was an unknown and had nothing going for him and everything working against him. Now everyone would see what he could do.

Not only would Gideon decisively win the battle against the foreign invaders and drive them out, but he also would go on to become Israel's next judge. As such, he went on to rule for the next forty years in peace. Not bad for a man who was wondering where his next meal would come from.

Likewise, God has something for you to do that no one else can do. He is calling forth some earth shakers and some history makers, some prophets and prophetesses, some business owners, some millionaires, some attorneys, and some first ladies.

It doesn't matter if you have a terrible past and you've done some things that you're ashamed of. You're a prime candidate for His glory.

Welcome to new beginnings. You will now begin to think differently, feel differently, and act differently. Your mind is being renewed, and your perceptions are changing. You don't have to stay on the sidelines any longer because God doesn't love any other person in the world more than He loves you.

Rebuke every spirit of confusion and despondency that have come against your life. Claim your freedom from insecurity and low self-esteem. Now, lift up your eyes unto the hills from where your help comes. You were made and created in the image of God, and you have a great destiny. As you move from insecurity to confidence, you can begin *Living the Dream.*

Chapter Four

LEARNING THAT YOU ARE WHO GOD SAYS YOU ARE

Let the wicked forsake his way, and the unrighteous man his thoughts; let him return to the LORD, and He will have mercy on him; and to our God, for He will abundantly pardon. "For My thoughts are not your thoughts, nor are your ways My ways," says the LORD.

Isaiah 55:7–8

You are who God says you are, and you must begin to believe it if you expect to live your dream.

Satan will do everything in his power to prevent that. He doesn't want you to grow into the man or woman that God ultimately wants you to be. So he puts many different enemies in your way to break your focus and take you off of your road to destiny. But if you press forward in the right direction, you can obtain every promise that God has ever made to you.

How you think totally affects how you live. If you continually think, *I'm the victim of circumstances*, then you may just become a victim of circumstances. But if you begin to think to the contrary: *I've been created by God, and all things are underneath my feet*, then you'll soon discover that all things will be beneath your feet.

When God said, *"Let the wicked forsake his way, and the unrighteous man his thoughts; let him return to the LORD,"* He meant more than we might at first think. This phrase, *"return to the LORD,"* refers to a moment when you forsake your own thoughts and embrace God's thoughts. That's the secret of your future. If you want power and dominion, you must believe that you are who God says you are.

The problem may be that the average person in the body of Christ doesn't know who God says he is. And if you don't know, the devil will try to define who you are. Avoiding the devil's definition is vital to your success, since whatever you think ultimately will be what you become.

As a pastor, it's disturbing to me to see people who have been Christians for many years still have deficient finances. It disturbs me when I see those who have been Christians for a long time not growing. They're simply maintaining their experience year after year. Personally, it's discouraging when I see human beings who have been created in the likeness and image of God, crowned with glory and honor, and to whom God has given power to have dominion, remain totally satisfied with unrewarding jobs, mediocre marriages, and half-hearted prayer lives.

When you begin to understand who you are in God, you're going to start thinking it. When you start thinking it, you're going to start acting it. And when you start acting it, you're going to become it.

God has placed us here on this earth to have dominion, not to live from paycheck to paycheck, barely making it and struggling for the rest of our lives. Some who are reading this are working right now on an unrewarding job—although perhaps not by choice. This concerns me because God has called me to help people grow from glory to glory. It's my job to help people stretch, to see what they can become.

That's what people need today. We need someone to prod us and cause us to reach out for more. And the sky is not even the limit, for God has much more for each of us.

It's not enough to say amen to some new revelation. God requires that we forsake our thoughts and accept His revelation. His thoughts are not our thoughts. He said it Himself: *"For My thoughts are not your thoughts, nor are your ways My ways."* He went on,

For as the heavens are higher than the earth, so are My ways higher than your ways, and My thoughts than your thoughts.
Isaiah 55:9

God is saying to us, "I really don't see you the way you see yourself." And He wants to use me in this book to help you see yourself as He sees you. When you begin to see yourself as God sees you, then your thinking is going to be different. You will understand that God has placed dominion on the inside of you.

When we get God's thoughts, then we will get God's ways. There is no sickness in heaven. There's no poverty. No one is struggling financially there. That's the type of order God has established in heaven, and He desires to see the same blessing within your life down here.

On a daily basis, the enemy will come to attack your thoughts. He wants you to think that where you are is where you always will be, that life will always be as it is today. He knows that if you think like that, you're going to live like that.

But there are some of you who know where you are in reality. You're just passing through this land. Some of you know right now that the ways things are in your life is not the way it always will be. You can't explain how God will do it, but you know that He will. You haven't been through all that you've been through for nothing. There is more on the way.

And when you get God's thoughts, you're suddenly on your way somewhere. You may not know where, but you always know that it's to a higher level.

If all that you embrace is what you hear on the news, you'll be in trouble. The average person who doesn't understand God's thoughts lives a mediocre lifestyle, and the most terrible thing about it is that he's satisfied with life as it is. Such a person might be heard to say:

"Hey, I got a good job. It's not much, but it's good enough. You know what I mean?"

"Hey, my father struggled, so why shouldn't I?"

"My family never had anything, so what makes me think I should have something?"

As long as you embrace thoughts such as these, you're going to have just what you're believing for. When you begin to talk differently (because you're thinking differently), things will change. You might begin to say, "Hey, wait a minute. Look at the way God has blessed these other people. And He doesn't love them anymore than He loves me. So I deserve to be blessed the same way they're blessed." And you will get it.

Learning That You Are Who God Says You Are

You are the very righteousness of God created in Christ Jesus. These may be "hard times," but there have been hard times before. In fact, there were hard times in the 1950s, there were hard times in the 1960s, and there were hard times in the 1970s, 80s, and 90s. We somehow thought that hard times would cease as we moved in to a new millennium, but it didn't happen. There always will be hard times, but that doesn't change God or His power. He can bless us in the midst of hard times.

God is saying to you today, "Understand the potential that exists on the inside of you." As I said before, if you can begin to think like who you are in God's sight, then you will start acting like it. And when you start acting like it, you will start seeing it come to pass in your life.

You have to start walking around like you're a child of the King. You have to start acting like you're the righteousness of God. Your boss is not your source; God is. Submit to those whom God has placed over you, but understand that promotion doesn't come from the east, the west, the north, or the south. Promotion comes from above. Only God can cause you to live your dream.

He has the power to transcend all conditions. Somebody might say, "Well, Bishop, you just don't understand. I'm doing fairly well, considering. You see, I don't have much education, and everyone is looking for well educated people these days."

Oh, you'd be surprised how many rich people don't have a good education.

Others might say, "Well, look at the color of my skin. I have too many strikes against me because I was born this way."

But there are many people with skin just like yours who are prospering and doing just fine in life.

Still others may say, "I'm just too old, Bishop."

That's not a legitimate excuse for failure either. I can show you plenty of people who are as old or older than you are, and they're doing just fine.

There are several other common excuses used as to why a person cannot do well in life. But if you have the proper attitude, absolutely nothing and no one can prevent you from becoming who God says you already are. You are the only one who can stop your progress, so you are your own worst enemy.

The prophet Jeremiah shows us how God thinks about us:

For I know the thoughts that I think toward you, says the LORD, thoughts of peace and not of evil, to give you a future and a hope.

Jeremiah 29:11

Wow! That's exciting. The Amplified Bible says it this way:

For I know the thoughts and plans I have for you, says the Lord, thoughts and plans for welfare and peace and not for evil, to give you hope in your final outcome.

"Your final outcome" is the realization of your dream. Can you sense how bright your future is? God is about to do some things for you that will just amaze you. He's saying to you today, "If you could just see what I'm about to do, then you would start acting like who you are about to become."

It doesn't matter if you don't have a dime in your pocket; you can still have dignity in your heart because you understand who you are and whose you are. The people of the world may not respect you yet because they don't know you yet. But give them an opportunity, and they will respect you too.

Learning That You Are Who God Says You Are

It doesn't matter how many strikes are against you; you are the righteousness of God, created in Christ Jesus. So start acting like it.

When I see all of the attacks the devil makes against me, it makes me realize just how important I am to God. If I were just a nobody, like the enemy claims, he wouldn't have reason to bother with me.

So why is he trying to kill us? Why is he trying to stop us? He knows that we can quickly become who God says we already are.

Many of us have had strikes against us since childhood, and the devil uses them every chance he gets. But why is he so intimidated by you? Why is he so afraid of you? There must be a reason. He's afraid that you're going to discover who you are in God. And when you find out who you are in God, every demon will have to submit to you.

Some may find this kind of talk arrogant, but it's not. When we declare that we are who God says we are, we're just saying what He's already said, and there's nothing arrogant about that.

Don't worry about how much you're earning right now. Don't worry about where you're living right now. Don't worry about what your job is right now. None of that matters, for you're on your way to greatness. There's a dream on the inside of you that's about to come forth.

Again, this kind of talk may not be well received by some. They are far too "realistic." Well, if you don't want to better your life, that's up to you. As for me, God has shown me who I am, and I don't plan to allow anything to stop me from achieving all that He has planned for me. He has shown me not only who I am, but also where I'm going and what He plans to do through me. So why should I settle for anything less?

If you will trust God today, your struggling days will soon be over. I promise you that. God is getting ready to give you the dominion that He has said is yours. You may be working for someone else, but He wants you to have people working for you. Start believing that you are about to take over, and you will.

Average believers never intimidate the enemy or threaten his kingdom because they're always busy wrestling with their own self-image. He says to them, "You've made so many mistakes in life that you'll never get what you're dreaming about," and they believe what he says and settle for second best. Please don't do that. Maintain a healthy self-image.

Get Over the Past

There are several things that will control your self-image if you let them. First, Satan uses your past. The past has many of us stuck in a rut, but God wants to deliver you from the past right now and give you a glorious future. Forget the past and accept God's tomorrows. A dark past means a bright future.

Most of our thoughts about ourselves in the present are based on what we were and what we did in the past. This could include either past failures or past successes.

People made bad comments about us in the past, and we have allowed their words to hinder us in the present. In the past we had some wrong teachings, and we have allowed those teachings to hinder us in the present day. In the past we did not always have the best examples to follow, and we have allowed that fact cloud our present and our future. The things of the past have too long decided who and what we are today, and it's time to be delivered from the past.

The events of your past have caused you to develop a certain thought pattern, and that thought pattern controls your present.

Learning That You Are Who God Says You Are

What you have been doesn't have to be what you will be. This is true even for good memories. Far too many people are so stuck on "the good old days" that they can't move forward. The truth is that when we remember "the good old days," we're probably exercising selective memory, only thinking of the good things that happened and forgetting everything else. Let God guide your thoughts, not memories—real or imagined.

It doesn't matter what type of car you might drive; you can't move forward if you're constantly looking in the rearview mirror. That rearview mirror has a purpose, and it's not to get you where you're going. Don't look back too long, or you'll never reach your destination. You'll never reach your future by always focusing on the past. It's a new day, so get on with life.

A rearview mirror has a limited usefulness when your car is moving forward, and you should only glance at it once in a while. Refuse to allow the devil to stop your forward motion because of what happened to you in the past.

Some people have the opposite type of selective recall. They can't remember any good days at all. According to them, they were all bad. They only remember rejection, insult, poverty, rape, and abuse. They only remember the day someone told them they were a nobody. They only remember someone saying that they were a mistake. They only remember someone saying, "Your daddy was nothing, and you're just like him." Some people actually relive the hurt caused by such insults over and over again and allow it to poison their lives.

It's time to see ourselves as God sees us. Forget the past—the good and the bad—and reach out for God's todays and tomorrows.

The past is passed. It's over. It's history. Let go of it. Chalk it up to a learning experience, and move on. Whatever you do, don't let your past dictate your future.

I'm not about to go back for any reason. Today is wonderful, and tomorrow will be even more wonderful.

The things that are behind you are just that—behind you. The people behind you are just that—behind you. Don't allow your past to damage your self-image.

The devil never reminds you of good things you've done. He reminds you of all the "mess-ups" and the "foul-ups." This is his way of making you feel undeserving and unworthy. Then, when something bad happens, your mind says to you, "That's just what I had coming to me. That's just what I deserved."

But the devil's a liar. God has said, *"My thoughts are not your thoughts, nor are your ways My ways,"* and before you even went through those terrible "messes" in recent years, He knew exactly what was going to happen. He could have prevented it if He had wanted to, but He didn't. He allowed you to go through the "mess" so that you would have a message of redemption for others. Refuse to be controlled by the past.

Let that divorce go. Let that abortion go. Let that hatred go. Let that relationship go. It's history. It's over. Now, move on.

What you experienced in your past has nothing at all to do with what God has planned for your future. So, let the past go. Forget about it. Bury it.

God said, *"Let the wicked forsake his way, and the unrighteous man his thoughts."* So stop thinking about it. Period!

When the devil tries to bring up my past, I bring up his past. When he tries to talk to me, I talk back to him. When he continues to bring up my past, I tell him what God has said about my future. And if he still doesn't leave me alone, I tell him what God has said about his future. That usually sends him running in pain.

Learning That You Are Who God Says You Are

Get a Vision for the Future

The second issue that will control your self-image is a lack of vision. Such a lack of vision will bring fear and pain into your life. It will bring doubt into your life. It will bring confusion into your life. God said,

Where there is no vision, the people perish.

Proverbs 29:18 KJV

God has placed great ability, or creative power, inside you. That potential is there. You just don't know who you are. You're destined to become a history maker and an earth shaker. But lack of vision will extinguish that flame.

Lack of vision will destroy your potential, so this is what you should do. In every area of your life, begin to think increase, target increase, and talk increase. Do that every day of the year. Every day see where you are going, target how you're going to get there, and then begin to tell everyone about it.

I'm no longer talking just about where I've been or where I presently am. I'm talking about where I'm going. I'm talking about what God has already shown me because I have a vision for the future.

Confess to others, "My finances are going to get better. My family is going to get better. My future is going to be better."

First, think it. Then, target it. And, finally, speak it out.

I hope you're getting excited about this because I am. Are you expecting increase? Expectation means that you begin acting as if your miracle has already happened. You consider it to be already done, as God does.

Once you have thought increase, targeted increase, and talked increase, keep saying it and saying it and saying it some more until you see it. If you keep on saying it, you will eventually see it.

You don't yet see yourself as God sees you, and He says to you today, "If you saw yourself the way I see you, you would be acting differently. You would be talking differently. Your whole life would be different."

Isaiah the prophet was used by God to say to us,

Do not remember the former things, nor consider the things of old. Behold, I will do a new thing, now it will spring forth; shall you not know it?

Isaiah 43:18–19

Things are about to get better, so start acting like it's already done. Personally, I refuse to move from my confession because I've already seen a preview of coming attractions. I already know where God is taking me, and that gives me faith.

Faith comes when you hear God talk, and you need to listen to Him. He talks to us by His Spirit, He talks to us through His servants, and He talks to us through the Holy Scriptures. What He is saying should encourage every one of us.

That's why, when we read the Bible, we get excited about it. God is talking to us, and He's showing us a greater tomorrow.

Many have heard the story of Ray Kroc. He was already past fifty and selling blenders to make milkshakes to support himself and his family. He was doing fairly well at that, but suddenly he had a vision of something else he thought might be even more successful. It was a chain of hamburger stores, and he called it McDonald's. The rest is history.

Learning That You Are Who God Says You Are

In his book *Grinding It Out,* Kroc tells that no one believed that he could really prosper in his venture because the economy was in a recession and taxes were too high. It was a difficult time to get ahead. There seemed to be no more opportunities in America. At least that was what everyone was saying. Then he founded his famous hamburger chain.

He wrote the book in 1977, and when he wrote it, people were saying the same things they had said when he had started his business years before. That's the way people are. They will tell you, "Oh, that can't be done," or "You can't do that."

There are always two camps—those who believe they can't and those who just do it. Who do you plan to listen to? Get a vision of a bright future and start working toward it—at whatever age you happen to be.

You can be sure that God has more in store for you than you are presently experiencing. And what He has is bigger than you. Actually, it's not really about you at all. It has nothing to do with you. When you're walking in divine destiny and purpose, what you do will bring glory to God. And you'll get a lot of joy from that.

Stop Comparing Yourself with Others

The third thing that will control your self-image is comparing yourself with others. You must believe that you are who God says you are and not allow anything to destroy that image for you.

You are a unique individual. You were created unlike anyone else, and therefore you cannot be compared to others. Paul wrote to the Corinthian church,

For we dare not class ourselves or compare ourselves with those who commend themselves. But they, measuring themselves by

themselves, and comparing themselves among themselves, are not wise.

2 Corinthians 10:12

Why is it that people are constantly comparing us with others? This is *"not wise,"* and there's no reason to do it.

The devil loves comparisons, but don't accommodate him. You are unique. When God made you, He didn't make any more from that same mold.

Every time you compare yourself to others, one of two things happens. You either put others down to lift yourself up, or you put yourself down by comparing yourself to others. And you don't want to do either of these.

Some examples of the first might be:

"I make more money than he does."

"My wife is prettier than his."

"My husband looks better than that."

"I can quote more verses than he can."

"I've got a better job than he does."

Some examples of the second might be:

"I wish I was as good as he."

"I'd love to be married to her."

"I wish I had a husband like that."

"Oh, if I only had a car like that one."

If we continue to do what's right, then everything that's wrong and everybody who's wrong will leave us. In the meantime, we have no reason to make comparisons. It doesn't help anyone.

Learning That You Are Who God Says You Are

Rather than make constant comparisons, simply believe that you are who God says you are. Successful people understand that no one makes it to the top in a single bound, so your delayed success doesn't mean that you are not on your way. Others have made it, so you can too.

So these three enemies come to haunt us and to keep us from moving into the future: the past, lack of vision, and comparisons with others. But if you can see yourself as God sees you, all of these enemies (and many others) will be conquered.

You are unique. There is something about you that God likes. This should be obvious to you. Just look at what you've been through. Look at how He has fed you and kept you. Look at all the others who have become victims, while He has allowed you to remain a victor.

Oh, yes, you have some scars, and you have some bad memories. But through it all, look at where you are today. Look at how good God has been to you, in spite of yourself. Look at the favor He has put upon your life. Look at how He has blessed you even in your times of disobedience. If He has blessed you like this, and you've been disobedient, can you imagine what He's going to do for you when you become totally obedient to Him?

In every situation, somebody has always been there to work things out for you. Somebody has always gone to bat for you. When people have tried to tear you down, somebody else has been there to build you up and speak well on your behalf. There is definitely something about you that God likes.

You're also an affront to the devil. He's very nervous because he knows that your thinking is now straightened out, and he knows that if you keep going in the direction you're going, you'll receive every promise that God has made to you.

LIVING THE DREAM

You're great in the opinion of God. You're somebody special. You're a chosen vessel. You're a vessel of honor made for the Master's use. Greatness is on the inside of you.

You're going so much further than where you are right now. You're going so much higher than you are at the moment. And it has nothing to do with you. The Lord will do it for you so that He may be glorified.

See yourself today as God sees you, and you will find yourself well on your way toward *Living the Dream*.

Chapter Five

LEARNING TO TAKE
WHAT'S ALREADY YOURS

And the LORD said: "I have surely seen the oppression of My peo-
ple who are in Egypt, and have heard their cry because of their
taskmasters, for I know their sorrows. So I have come down to
deliver them out of the hand of the Egyptians, and to bring
them up from that land to a good and large land, to a land
flowing with milk and honey, to the place of the Canaanites and
the Hittites and the Amorites and the Perizzites and the Hivites
and the Jebusites."

Exodus 3:7–8

Whenever we're studying any passage of scripture, there are
three questions that we must ask ourselves: What did it mean
then? What does it mean now? And what does it mean to me personally? When we ask ourselves those three questions, then the

Word of God becomes alive within us. The revelation literally explodes into our spirits.

Everything written in the Bible is there for a reason, but some things had a certain meaning back then, and they don't mean the same today. We want to know what they mean to us as a people and also as individuals.

God said some wonderful things to the children of Israel in this particular passage. He said that He had heard their prayer, that He had come down to deliver them out of the hand of the Egyptians, and that He had come to bring them into a good and large land, a land flowing with milk and honey. How does that apply to me today? That land is mine, and I intend to claim every inch of it.

Later, in Numbers 13, we find the execution of the promise that God had made. It did come to pass because He said it would. And if He speaks a thing, that's enough. We can count on it, because if He said it, it will come to pass. There is a promised land waiting for each of us.

The Wilderness

When the time came for the actual possession of the land, the children of Israel were where many of us find ourselves right now; they were in the wilderness. But although their lives appeared bleak at the moment, they were very near to the land God had promised. In fact, they were just on it.

Many of us are going through a wilderness right now, but we must continue to trust God because we're closer than we've ever been to the land that flows with milk and honey. What did it mean then? What does it mean now? What does it mean to me personally?

Learning to Take What's Already Yours

Often, when we get close to what God has promised us, suddenly all hell seems to break loose. You know what I'm talking about. Suddenly, the land around us seems more barren than ever. Everything seems to have dried up. In reality, we're just within striking distance of the Promised Land, but we don't know it, so we allow ourselves to become discouraged.

We must not let this happen—ever. The land is ours, and it's time to move in and take possession of it.

God had spoken of a land flowing with milk and honey, and they were now very near to it, but what they were seeing was not milk and honey at all.

Still, if God said it, it was sure. He didn't have to swear. He did not have to cross His heart and hope to die. If He said it, that was enough.

What does the Promised Land mean to you? It surely doesn't mean that you'll be moving to Israel, but God has a promised land right where you are.

Please don't despair in the wilderness. You're almost to the Promised Land. And don't despise what you are presently going through. It has a purpose. It is getting you ready to conquer the land.

The Milk

When God promised milk and honey, He knew what He was doing. Milk is one of the necessities of life, and God was saying that He would supply all of the people's needs. He is so awesome that He has placed a milk supply in every female mammal so that she can nurture her little ones. What a miracle that is!

Think of it. When a female dog is about to have pups, suddenly her body begins to change, and she produces a milk that is perfectly balanced for their consumption.

LIVING THE DREAM

The body of the female cat likewise undergoes a change, and she suddenly has milk to feed her litter of kittens. This is such an amazing phenomenon, and God does it.

A mother bear produces milk in her body for her cubs, and a human mother does the same thing. The changes that come over a woman are dramatic, as God prepares her to nurture her little one.

Another remarkable thing about this process is that it doesn't happen at any other time, only when it's needed. I find that to be so awe-inspiring, and I'm sure that you do too.

Every child needs milk, and God has made provision for it. Milk is a necessity.

God was saying to the children of Israel, "I will bring you into a land that flows with all the necessities of life. When you get into this land, everything you need will flow to you." Oh, I like that. That's what our God is like. This caused David to sing,

The LORD is my shepherd; I shall not want.
Psalm 23:1

What did it mean then? What does it mean now? And what does it mean to me personally? If there is any lack in our lives, it shows that we have not yet moved into the land, for when we get there, all lack will vanish. There, we will have need of nothing. We will no longer have to live from paycheck to paycheck. We will no longer have to struggle to get by.

I'm not talking about some pie in the sky in some sweet bye and bye. I'm talking about the here and now. God wants to do this for us *now*.

That land is yours. Claim it and move into it.

Learning to Take What's Already Yours

The Honey

But God went further. Not only would they have milk, the necessities of life, flowing to them in this land; they would have something else as well. This land would not only flow with milk; it would also flow with honey.

Although milk is a necessity, we can live without ever tasting honey. Milk is something we all need, but honey is something that we don't particularly need. It's a delicacy.

Still, God says that because of what we've been through, not only will He meet our needs, but He will also give us the things we want. And now's the time. Let it flow.

Milk is a necessity, but honey is a nicety. When I first said that, I wasn't even sure *nicety* was a word, but it sounded good to me. God will not only give us what we need, but also what we want. That's the God we're serving.

Stop making apologies for the way God is blessing you. When we're obedient to Him, He will bring us into milk and honey, and we don't have to apologize to anyone for that.

Let me give you an example. Clothing is a necessity. That's the milk of the Promised Land. We all need clothes. Shoes are a necessity. Shelter is a necessity. And God has promised to provide all of those things.

But when He gives you several pairs of shoes, and in different colors, to match the many dresses He's provided, that's pure honey. We don't need many pairs of shoes. They are not an absolute necessity of life.

You women don't need a green dress, a red dress, a blue dress, a yellow dress, and a black dress. That's honey. When God gives us the second and the third and the fourth, then we can know that we've gone beyond the essentials and are into the extra blessings He has promised.

A purse might be considered a necessity, but a Gucci purse would certainly have to be categorized as honey. You need clothes, but they don't have to be designer clothes. God, however, wants to do for us not just the bare minimum—He wants to do much more. He has promised us not only what we need, but also what we want.

When you go to God in prayer and you need a car, it's not wrong to be specific and ask Him to give you a particular model of car. As for shelter, all you need is a roof over your head, but God wants to go beyond that. He wants to bless you with room enough so that you can have a quiet place to study and pray.

I'm saying all of this because we need to change our way of thinking when it comes to what God wants us to have. Stop thinking that He wants you to struggle to have the bare necessities of life. He's not happy when you're just getting by. The land is yours, and it's not wrong to take it.

I'm on my way to that land, and I hope you are too. God said that I could have it, so I'm going to take it. It's already mine, and I'm just laying claim to what is mine.

You can't stop me from going into the land because God said that I could have it. That's where He wants me to be. He has provided it for me. So our best days are just ahead of us.

The Spies

As the children of Israel were preparing to cross over into the Promised Land, Moses sent out some men to spy out the land. I'm sure that he must have reminded them of the promises given by God earlier. They were to go into the land and bring back some evidence. Moses wanted to let the people know that God always kept His word. What happened there was amazing:

> *Then they came to the Valley of Eshcol, and there cut down a branch with one cluster of grapes; they carried it between two of them on a pole. They also brought some of the pomegranates and the figs. The place was called the Valley of Eshcol, because of the cluster which the men of Israel cut down there. And they returned from spying out the land after forty days.*
>
> Numbers 13:23–25

When the spies reached a place later called the Valley of Eshcol, they saw a cluster of grapes so large that it would require two of them to carry it. They cut it and carried it back on a pole between two men. That sounds like my land.

The Grapes

How big did that cluster of grapes have to be that it required two men to carry it? This was their evidence—those huge grapes, those wonderful figs, those delicious pomegranates. Here was the proof. God had said that it was a good land, and this was proof that He had told the truth.

Can you imagine the excitement in the camp when the spies got back bearing those grapes? I can hear people saying, "I've never seen grapes that big in all my life."

For forty days, the spies had searched through the land on the other side of Jordan, and now they were back, they had the evidence they had sought, and everyone was excited about it. Now, the Promised Land was no longer just a dream. The reality of it had been manifested.

LIVING THE DREAM

Let me tell you something today. The life you're about to live—within a very short period of time—will surprise and thrill and excite you. And you won't be the only one who's surprised. Your enemies also will be surprised. They will wonder how you suddenly became so blessed.

Suddenly, the children of Israel were rejoicing and giving each other high fives. They were excited because the evidence of what God had spoken was now there before them. They could all see it with their own eyes. The land was surely waiting for them, and it was indeed a land of bounty.

The spies were obedient and brought back the evidence for all to see:

> Now they departed and came back to Moses and to Aaron and all the congregation of the children of Israel in the Wilderness of Peran, at Kadesh; they brought back word to them and to all the congregation, and showed them the fruit of the land. Then they told him [Moses], and said: "We went to the land where you sent us. It truly flows with milk and honey, and this is its fruit."
>
> Numbers 13:26–27

When God gives you a word, you can take it to the bank. He cannot lie, and He will not lie. So you can begin shouting and rejoicing immediately. You can begin to place your sights on the land, knowing that He is about to give it to you.

The Giants

But the spies had some other news, and it was not so good. The people had rejoiced to see the grapes, the evidence of the promise, but there was more. Someone among the spies was not rejoicing, or rather most of the spies, it turned out, were not rejoicing. "Stop the music," someone was saying. "Stop the dancing. Stop the shouting and rejoicing. There's more to the story." They went on:

Nevertheless the people who dwell in the land are strong; the cities are fortified and very large; moreover we saw the descendants of Anak there. The Amalakites dwell in the land of the South; the Hittites, the Jebusites, and the Amorites dwell in the mountains; and the Canaanites dwell by the sea and along the banks of the Jordan.

Numbers 13:28–29

Yes, it was a land flowing with milk and honey, and the fruit they had brought back proved it, but there was a catch. The land was already occupied, and the occupants were not normal people; they were giants. This terrified the majority of the spies and they were sure that the plan to take the land should be abandoned.

But not all of the spies were so pessimistic. Caleb spoke out now:

Then Caleb quieted the people before Moses, and said, "Let us go up at once and take possession, for we are well able to overcome it."

Numbers 13:30

"What's the big deal?" Caleb was saying. "It's no problem. Yes, I saw the giants too, but if God has said that this is our land, then we can go in and possess it. What are we waiting for? Let's go take it now!"

Joshua agreed with Caleb, but the people became unsure of what they should do when they saw that a majority of the spies had a very different attitude about this undertaking:

75

But the men who had gone up with him said, "We are not able to go against the people, for they are stronger than we." And they gave the children of Israel a bad report of the land which they had spied out, saying, "The land through which we have gone as spies is a land that devours its inhabitants, and all the people whom we saw in it are men of great stature. There we saw the giants (the descendants of Anak came from the giants); and we were like grasshoppers in our own sight, and so we were in their sight."

Numbers 13:31–33

So where did they stand now? The group had come back bearing the fruit that proved God's promise to be true, but ten of the twelve now insisted that the land could not be taken. The others wanted to rejoice, but these ten insisted that all rejoicing stop for the moment because there was a serious problem.

Caleb and Joshua didn't agree. They were in favor of going in at once and taking the land. "We can do it," they insisted. But what should the people do now that they knew there were giants in the land?

Our promised land will always be infested with giants, and we will never be able to take them without a fight. This happens because, when God makes us a promise, the devil will do everything in his power to keep it from coming to pass. He's not going to just stand by and let you easily take what is yours without a fight.

When you find yourself going though all sorts of torments, know that it's because the giants in your promised land are trying to prevent you from laying your hands on what is already yours. But the very fact that they're fighting you shows that you are near to victory. You're almost there. Any day now, you will possess your promised land.

Learning to Take What's Already Yours

Personally, I can say that there are always a lot of giants hanging around my grapes. I know what God has promised me, but to get to it, I always have to deal with the giants who stand in my way.

Don't be afraid to deal with your giants—the giants on your job, the giants in your house, the giants who try to devour your money. Face them boldly, for if God has said that the land is yours, then it's yours.

But why would God tell us that the land was ours, if He knew all along that it was full of giants? Why are there giants in my promised land? I know what God has promised me, and I can sense in my spirit that it's all true, but now the devil is telling me that it will never happen because there are too many giants in the way and I can't get around them.

Why are those giants there? They're there because God knew if all I had to do was just stroll up and take the grapes, I wouldn't need Him. If it was like that, many of us wouldn't be going to church or praying or seeking God through His Word. We wouldn't need Him any longer.

If this happened, we would have grapes, but no God. So He puts the grapes in our promised land, but He also allows giants to be placed in our way so that we need Him to help us get to our grapes.

If God said that we can eat the grapes, then we can—regardless of who or what seems to stand in our way. We'll deal with the giants, and we'll prevail, because God is on our side.

Some of you have a giant as a spouse. Some of have a giant as a boss. Some of you have a giant as a parent. Some of you have a giant as a neighbor. Your ex-wife (or ex-husband) may be your giant. Anybody at all could be a giant in your life.

Your sickness may be your giant. Your financial situation may be your giant. Your lack of education may be your giant. But none of that changes God. He said that the land was yours, so it's yours. That's all there is to it.

Don't worry about the giants. It doesn't matter how big they are. The God we serve is bigger than any giant is.

Some are satisfied with the way life is, and they would rather stay in the wilderness than fight giants. Probably nothing I could say would ever change them. But there are others who know that God has more in store for them. They're not ashamed to proclaim to their neighbors that they intend to go for the grapes.

They're not worried about giants. They're concentrating on those grapes, and whatever they have to go through to get to where God wants them to be, they're willing. The land is theirs, and they intend to take it.

Well, let your neighbors who are satisfied in the wilderness take a good look at you now, for where you are now is not where you always will be. You know what God has promised you, and you're not willing to settle for anything less. You're bound for the Promised Land, and nothing will prevent you from reaching it.

If you don't want more, if your life is wonderful enough already, and everything is just the way you want it to be, you can just opt out of the fight with the giants and live like you want to. But please excuse the rest of us. We have some giants to fight and some land to possess.

We're not there yet, but we're on our way. There are grapes and there are giants, and the latter will not prevent us from having the former.

The Grasshoppers

The giants of Canaan were not easily dismissed, and when the ten spies saw them, they suddenly felt like grasshoppers. But notice something very important. The grapes were real, and the giants were real, but the grasshoppers were only imagined. This was just a metaphor for the way the spies felt at the moment. Being grasshoppers was not a reality. It was just their current mind-set.

If you see yourself as a grasshopper, the devil will begin to address you as one. He knows that if he can make you believe you are one, you will become one. But you're not a grasshopper. You can do all things through Christ. So make up your mind to go for your grapes. If God said you could have them, then you must believe that you can and will.

Taking the Land

Dealing with giants can be very unpleasant, but our God is a big God. That land is mine, and I'm going for it. I'm willing to deal with the giants. The bigger they are, the harder they fall. If God be for me, who can be against me?

God has said,

Every place that the sole of your foot will tread upon I have given you.

Joshua 1:3

Don't be ashamed or afraid to declare that the land is yours. Begin to talk like it's yours, and begin to act like it's yours. Your period of living from hand to mouth is just about over. No weapon formed against you can prosper, so go for your grapes. Dry your eyes and stop your crying. Victory is at hand.

It's yours, so take it. Healing is yours. Prosperity is yours. That husband or wife you have been needing is waiting for you in your promised land. That job you have needed is waiting for you there. God has promised you great things. They're yours.

Your breakthrough is coming. You'll find everything you need in your promised land. Start praising God for it right now.

Stop worrying about the giants, and go after your grapes.

Oh, it's no wonder you've been having so many battles. Those giants don't want to relinquish the land, but it's yours. Take it.

You don't have to wait until the battle's over. Start praising God now. Shout now! Get rid of your grasshopper mentality and start eating from the land. If God is on your side, what else do you need?

When you begin to take what is already yours, you set yourself on the path toward *Living the Dream*.

Chapter Six

LEARNING TO RECOGNIZE YOUR FULL POTENTIAL

Now to Him who is able to do exceedingly abundantly above all that we ask or think, according to the power that works in us. To Him be glory in the church by Christ Jesus to all generations, forever and ever. Amen.

Ephesians 3:20–21

A true story was told by Dr. Bill Bright of a poor family named Yates who ran a small sheep ranch in rural Texas. The family struggled to keep food on the table, doing all they could to survive, but they had to accept government assistance or lose both their home and their land to the creditors.

One day, in the midst of this bleakness, a representative from a large oil company came knocking at the door. He said that his company wanted to drill a wildcat well on their property, and he promised a large portion of the profits if they should strike oil.

Mr. Yates and his wife talked it over. "Honey, what do I have to lose?" he said to her. *What could I lose?* he was thinking to himself. So he signed the papers.

The oil crew soon set up their machinery and began drilling. They drilled five hundred feet, and then eight hundred feet, and then a thousand feet, and still they had not hit anything. Then, at a little more than eleven hundred feet down, they tapped into one of the richest oil reserves yet discovered in the state of Texas.

Suddenly the well was spraying its black wealth high into the air, and soon it was pumping eighty thousand barrels of oil a day. Overnight, the Yates family became millionaires. Their property had been known as Yates' Field, but it now became known as Yates' Pool.

What had changed? Before, the Yates family had lived in poverty because they had not tapped into what they already owned. Some vast resources were beneath the surface of their farmland, but they did not yet know it.

You see, Mr. Yates had been a millionaire for quite some time, but he just didn't realize it. He had all of that untapped potential.

Many of us are just like the Yates family. We struggle along at the spiritual poverty level, all the while unaware of the vast resources that God has placed at our disposal. He has given us a plentiful reserve of resources.

It's in you—everything that is necessary for you to live the way God has destined you to live. You don't have to go looking for it because it's already in you. If you will just allow the Spirit of God to serve as your spiritual oil drill, He will help you tap into the resources that are already yours.

Learning to Recognize Your Full Potential

He can give us *"exceedingly abundantly above all that we can ask or think."* This promise really gets my attention because I can ask for some big things. I can think of some great goals. And the Lord is saying that whatever we can imagine can be ours—and more. It's already in us.

Most of us are walking around loaded down with something called potential, but we never use it. Or we use only a small portion of it. Whatever your mind conceives, you can do, and you can do it well. God will help you to do more than you could possibly imagine.

You can do what your mentors have never achieved. It's in you, because the Word of God says that He is able to do *"exceedingly abundantly above."* Exceedingly abundantly above what? Exceedingly abundantly above *all that you can ask or think*. Wow! That's powerful.

We can't do it in ourselves, but *"according to the power that works in us."*

There are paths awaiting you that no one has ever walked before. There are seeds of greatness in you that have not yet taken root.

Don't settle down where you happen to be today, don't get discouraged because you have had a setback or two, and don't give up just because a door has closed. Look for a window to open. Make up your mind. If God said that you can have something, then you can have it. It's in you.

Many Christians don't yet understand where they've come from, and if we don't know where we've come from, we can never understand where we're going. Understanding your history helps you navigate your future.

Say to the enemy of your soul, "Devil, you can try to keep me down, but I know this is in me." Some of you have known it since you were little children. You knew somehow that you were different from all of your other classmates and friends. They thought you were rather strange, and even you had to wonder if something might be wrong with you. You never seemed to fit in with the crowd.

It takes many people a lifetime to discover what's inside of them. Some, at thirty, forty, fifty, and older, are just now discovering who they are.

I would not waste my time telling you this if I were not convinced of it. You are a person of greatness. The proof is that you've been going through some struggles recently. The enemy knows that your destiny is about to surface, so he's desperately trying to knock you down. But this is your hour.

If the devil could have killed me, he would have. He gave it his best punch, but I'm still here. And I still have visions, goals, and dreams. There have been some setbacks, but that hasn't discouraged me. He has sometimes knocked me down, but he made a mistake when he didn't knock me out.

Creation Proves Potential

It's time for you to do what's never been done. The potential is in you. The very Creation proves it:

Then God said, "Let the earth bring forth grass, the herb that yields seed, and the fruit tree that yields fruit according to its kind, whose seed is in itself, on the earth"; and it was so. And the earth brought forth grass, the herb that yields seed according to its kind, and the tree that yields fruit, whose seed is in itself according to its kind.

Genesis 1:11–12

Learning to Recognize Your Full Potential

The grasses, the herbs, and the fruit trees were all created with the potential within themselves for reproducing their own kind.

So God created great sea creatures and every living thing that moves, with which the waters abounded, according to their kind, and every winged bird according to its kind.

Genesis 1:21

The creatures of the sea and the birds also were given potential to produce according to their kind.

Then God said, "Let the earth bring forth the living creature according to its kind: cattle and creeping thing and beast of the earth, each according to its kind"; and it was so. And God made the beast of the earth according to its kind, cattle according to its kind, and everything that creeps on the earth according to its kind.

Genesis 1:24–25

The beasts of the earth also were given this wonderful potential to produce after their kind. Finally, after creating many other things, God arrived at the moment He had long awaited. He was about to produce His crowning glory:

Then God said, "Let Us make man in Our image, according to Our likeness; let him have dominion...."

Genesis 1:26

Everything else in creation had the ability to reproduce after its kind, so God wanted something He could reproduce after His kind. He wanted to reproduce Himself. It was then that He said, *"Let Us make man...."* You are a reflection of God, and He has placed in you a vast potential.

When God made us humans, He did not make us from something that had never existed before. He made us of the same material of which He Himself was made. He said, "Let Me—Elohim, God of Creation, God with the power to call those things which be not as though they were, the Lord of lords, the King of kings, the Almighty God—make man, and when I do, I will put within him the same thing that I'm made of." That excites me.

This means that God created everything with potential. Every bird was created with the potential of reproducing more birds. Every gorilla has in it the ability to produce another gorilla—every snake, every cow, every baboon, every flower, every plant of any kind, every eagle, every buzzard, every duck, every fly, every ant...everything that God created, He created with potential. That potential is in you.

Just What Is Potential?

What is potential? Potential can be defined as unexposed ability. You have the ability, but it just hasn't been exposed yet.

What is potential? Potential is reserved power. There is a reserve of power in you.

What is potential? Potential is untapped strength. You have untapped strength in you.

What is potential? Potential is capped capabilities. You're capable of doing great things, but your capabilities are still capped, or sealed.

What is potential? Potential is hidden talent. There is some hidden talent in you. There's something unique that you can do, but the opportunity has never yet presented itself. Consequently, you don't know that you can do it. But that doesn't change the fact that you can.

What is potential? Potential is the sum of who you are that is yet to be revealed.

Learning to Recognize Your Full Potential

It's time for you to walk tall in the spirit. Others may not know you yet. They only see where you've been or where you are now, but they can't see where you're going. You have some potential in you that they haven't yet spotted.

For the moment, you may need to sit back and be obedient to those who are over you, but your day is coming. You're somebody whom even your friends and loved ones don't know yet. You'll surprise them all.

They don't know the real you, and that's why they treat you badly sometimes. That's why they overlook your talents. That's why they fail to give you opportunities. They don't mean anything bad by it; they just don't know who you are yet.

If they really knew you, they would be different in their attitude and their actions toward you. They're looking at what your present income level is. They're looking at what your present position is. They're looking at your current condition. They don't really know you because there's a you that's still hidden and has not yet been revealed.

The As-Yet-to-Be-Revealed You

There's a you that no one seems to know about. There's a you that no man has seen yet. There's a you that's about to rise to the occasion. Your capped capabilities are about to be uncapped. The top is about to be blown off of your well.

Everything that you have been through has been part of the manufacturing process to bring you to where you are today, so that your true potential can come out.

It's always been there. That's why the accident you suffered didn't kill you. That's why the abortion your mother tried to

87

have performed failed to wipe you out. That potential was always there.

The devil should have killed you when he had the chance, before you found out who you really were. You're capable of much more than you're presently thinking and much more than you're imagining. You're capable of doing more than you're presently doing, and you're capable of being more than you're presently being. You need to get this revelation into your spirit.

Say to yourself, "I'm about to become the real me. I haven't been me yet because I didn't know who I was. But when I looked at my history, I saw my future." Potential. It's in you.

Don't fail this test. You are about to become you. The big things that you only dreamed of before are now within your reach. The things that you only imagined are about to be manifested. It's time to get out of the boat because, if you never get out of the boat, you'll never be able to walk on the water. This is your time.

Don't "sell out," as we say, meaning, don't settle for second best. It doesn't matter how old you are. It doesn't matter how many mistakes you've made. It doesn't matter how small your thoughts have been in the past. Greatness is in your spirit right now.

As we have seen, when Genesis gives the account of the creation of the birds, of the creatures of the sea, and of the beasts of the field, it showed that all of them were created with potential. God would not have created something just so that it could exist. Everything in creation had a purpose and a potential, and that includes you.

We know how Genesis started with what we call *the beginning*:

In the beginning God created the heavens and the earth.

Genesis 1:1

88

Learning to Recognize Your Full Potential

But that was not really "the beginning." As we saw in the Introduction to the book, God existed before that time. If the book of Genesis had started with verse 0, it would have read like this: *"Before there was a beginning, there was God. Before there was a creation, there was a Creator. Before anything was, God existed."*

God didn't begin with the beginning. He didn't begin when the beginning began, for He was the beginning before the beginning had a beginning. Everything that was and is was in God at the beginning—or before.

Before God created anything, there was only God, so everything we see and everything we come in contact with came out of Him. Therefore, God had within Himself the potential for everything He made. Nothing exists that was not first in Him.

He said that the birds would produce other birds, the cattle would produce other cattle, and the other creatures would produce other creatures. And when He said, "I'm now going to make man, who will be created in My image," He was really saying, "Man will have the potential within himself to create as I have created. He can forfeit the opportunity, but it's there."

Some may disagree, but here's what I believe God's attitude toward you is; here's what I believe He's saying to you right now: "If you only knew who you were, you could do so much more. If you only knew what you could do, you would be amazed. If you only knew why I gave you life, you would not be wasting your time with trifles."

That said, would you like to know why you were created? Wouldn't you like to know why you have been going through so many trials? Wouldn't you like to know why you have undergone such special preparation?

If you ever discover who you are, look out. Yates was a millionaire living in poverty, and you may be too.

LIVING THE DREAM

Marry Potential to Vision

Potential, in order to produce something, must be married to vision. Potential with no vision remains only potential. If you have vision with no potential, you're just dreaming. But if you let your potential marry vision, you will give birth to destiny.

The prophet Habakkuk said,

> *I will stand my watch and set myself on the rampart, and watch to see what He will say to me, and what I will answer when I am corrected. Then the LORD answered me and said: "Write the vision and make it plain on tablets, that he may run who reads it. For the vision is yet for the appointed time; but at the end it will speak, and it will not lie. Though it tarries, wait for it; because it will surely come, it will not tarry."*
>
> Habakkuk 2:1–3

Is it possible to *"watch"* what someone says? Should he not have said, "I will 'listen' for what He will tell me." But, no, he said that he would watch to see what the Lord would say to him. Get your eyes open too.

You will no doubt see things that have not yet materialized, but don't worry about it. It's because your vision is still young. Your potential is still a teenager. Allow it to mature to the point that it can be married.

There is a suitable partner for your potential, and it is vision. When your potential and your vision come together, then you will become the you God destined you to be.

Can you see it? Can you see what God is about to do? Can you see what He has promised you? Something on the inside of you is great, and it's about to come to the surface. Everything that God promised will then come to pass. It's on the way. *"Though it tarries, wait for it; because it shall surely come."*

Learning to Recognize Your Full Potential

You are chock full of potential, and when that potential is married to vision, you can begin to shout—even when things seem to be at a standstill. You can say, "This is where I am now, but this is not where I will end up. God has already shown it to me, and I'm calling forth my greatness."

It's time to get out of the boat and walk on the water, for if God says you can have it, then you can have it. It doesn't matter what color your skin is. It doesn't matter who will try to stop you. Your best days, your proudest moments, are just ahead. Your enemies haven't seen anything yet. They have no idea of what God has put on the inside of you.

To every preacher, I say, "Your best sermons have not yet been preached." To every musician, I say, "Your greatest melodies have not yet been played." To every singer, I say, "Your greatest songs have not yet been sung." There is still great potential within each of you.

Get ready to deliver this baby, and don't miscarry. It's time.

I pity the preachers who have no idea what to preach in times like these. I pity the believer who has no testimony in times like these. I pity the soloist who doesn't have a song in times like these.

You'd better tell everyone around you, "Take a good look at me because I'm going through a process, and this time next year, I'll no longer be what I now am. I know it because the devil has been fighting me so hard."

You are about to explode with potential, so I command you, in the name of Jesus, get out of the boat. Everywhere you tread, the Lord will give you the land. It's yours for the asking.

And your enemies can't stop you. As the Lord has said,

"No weapon formed against you shall prosper, and every tongue which rises against you in judgment you shall condemn. This is

LIVING THE DREAM

the heritage of the servants of the LORD, and their righteousness is from Me," says the LORD.

Isaiah 54:17

Greatness is in you. Status is in you. Debt-free living is in you. Victory over sin is in you. Give birth to your purpose. It's in you!

Potential, capped capabilities, reserved power, unexposed ability, untapped strength… It's all in you. You don't have to wait for it. It's there. Begin to use it.

Some of you have no idea you are as strong as you are. Your real strength will be seen when you have been through some hot water, just like a tea bag.

The Lord is about to give you joy for all your bitterness and all your struggles. For weeks now, the enemy has thrown his best at you, attacking your mind and your body, but there is potential on the inside of you, and he cannot prevail.

You're not a follower; you're a leader. You've always been a leader.

Many of you have been dealing with internalized frustration that comes out as anger. That frustration is often caused by the fact that you have a vision, and things are not happening the way you thought they should happen. Your hurts and disappointments manifest as anger, but this only shows that on the inside of you is some untapped power, some capped capabilities. The cap is coming off, and it's time for you to fly high. It's time for you to take what the devil meant for evil and turn it around, as God is going to work it out for your good.

There is potential welling up on the inside of you. Sometimes you feel like you're about to smother. Let it out—all of your frustration, all of your hurt, all of your pain. Let it out. Be free!

Learning to Recognize Your Full Potential

Everything that God created, He created with potential, and as you work toward developing your God-given potential, you will begin *Living the Dream.*

LIVING THE DREAM

Chapter Seven

LEARNING TO BATTLE DEPRESSION

For though we walk in the flesh, we do not war according to the flesh. For the weapons of our warfare are not carnal [they're not physical or fleshly] *but mighty in God for pulling down strongholds.*

2 Corinthians 10:3–4

God truly anointed and used the apostle Paul to write not only to the church of Corinth, but also to us. God is doing a unique work within the lives of His people today, and He's doing it by His Spirit.

There's a war going on, and although we're still living in our fleshly bodies, we're no longer warring *"according to the flesh."* We have some spiritual weapons.

We all understand how important weapons are in the natural, and the events of recent years have proven how effective modern weapons can be. We need to believe God for some powerful weapons that we can use for His glory in the days ahead.

But many members of the body of Christ don't even know that they're in a battle. It's time that we put them on notice. With every step that we take in our walk with God, the enemy is attacking us spiritually. If we are unaware of the existence of the spiritual world, then we're already defeated.

Many of us know what it is to be attacked by the spirit of depression. Depression is a spirit, and it's one of the most common spirits the enemy sends against those of us who are born-again believers. Our chief enemies are often depression and discouragement. It doesn't matter who you are, what your title is, or how many scriptures you can quote (or even how vast your knowledge of God may be), you're still not immune to an attack of depression. Many of us know firsthand what it's like to be attacked by this evil spirit, so we've been there and experienced that, and we must warn others.

Depression attacks young and old alike, and it is so common today that I don't think we require a definition of it. It might be helpful, though, to have a description of what it's like. Depression is a feeling of helplessness and hopelessness that leads to a deep sadness. This malady strikes both men and women.

Some of you who are reading this will need this message today; those who don't can lay it away for a future time. But you will eventually need it. I guarantee it. God not only wants to speak to you today and show you how to personally overcome depression, but He also wants to use you as an instrument to get this message into the hands of others who are experiencing the same thing. Please obey Him.

Learning to Battle Depression

A person who is depressed has problems, but those problems may be either real or imagined. Many of the problems that people in depression dwell on in their minds are not easily identifiable, for they're not tangible. They may exist only in the mind. But whether the problems are real or imagined, a person suffering from depression cannot seem to get a handle on them. They feel bombarded with problems on every hand.

Another indication of depression is that there seems to be no one who can help the person who is suffering. This only compounds such people's fears. Not only are they in this situation, not only are they trying to deal with overwhelming problems (and usually being defeated), but they can't see any help arriving in the near future.

When we experience this feeling, we sometimes pray, "Lord, this situation has now gone from bad to worse. What will I do now? This may be the day I go under."

Many people have been attacked by a spirit of depression so frequently that they're walking around depressed and don't even know it. Some have been depressed for so long that they think this is just the way they are. Oh, my friend, I have good news: *The weapons of our warfare are not carnal but mighty in God for pulling down strongholds."* You can be free from the spirit of depression.

What does the Bible mean by this word *stronghold*? A stronghold, as we understand it in this context, is a mind-set that accepts a situation as being unchangeable, even though that situation may be contrary to the will of God. This has happened to men and women throughout the ages.

Let me show you from the Scriptures several people who experienced depression and what happened as a result of their depression. But before I do, let me say that depression is spiritual, and if you cannot learn how to deal with this spiritual enemy, you will live in constant defeat.

Moses Was Depressed

So Moses said to the LORD, "Why have You afflicted Your servant? And why have I not found favor in Your sight, that You have laid the burden of all of these people on me? Did I conceive all these people? Did I beget them, that You should say to me, 'Carry them in your bosom, as a guardian carries a nursing child,' to the land which You swore to their fathers? Where am I to get meat to give to all these people? For they weep all over me, saying, 'Give us meat, that we may eat.' I am not able to bear all these people alone, because the burden is too heavy for me. If You treat me like this, please kill me here and now—if I have found favor in Your sight—and do not let me see my wretchedness!"

Numbers 11:11–15

Listen to Moses pouring out his heart. He was obviously under a very heavy burden of depression. He was saying, "Lord, I didn't ask for this, and I can't handle it. Just kill me now, and don't make me suffer anymore."

It would be impossible for us to feel all that Moses was feeling at that moment, but we can imagine some of it. It's hard to lead any large group of people, and now the members of his group were complaining about their food. Moses didn't know what to tell them. Where was he going to get food for so many people? Would they die in the wilderness and he be blamed for it? Hear his heart. He was a desperate man.

Learning to Battle Depression

This was real life, and many of us have had similar experiences. We need not be ashamed to admit that we've been there—some of us many times over.

"Lord, this is too much for me."

"I can't bear this."

"These people are too much for me."

This burden is just too heavy for me to bear."

If you've never been there, I would be very surprised.

But when something like this happens, we suddenly find out how small we really are. Moses was suddenly so overwhelmed and so overburdened that he asked the Lord to kill him. This was just too much to bear. That's real life.

If we would be honest with God and with ourselves, we would have to admit that most of us know firsthand what this experience is like. Most of us, at one point or another in our lives, have gotten to the place that we didn't think life was worth living. Suddenly, life didn't meet our approval, and we wanted to stop the world and get off.

Could it be that the great Moses, who was called by God to deliver the people of Israel from bondage in Egypt, became so depressed that he wanted to die? Yes, it happened. The constant demands of the people became more than he could bear, and he didn't know how to help them.

A deep sadness had come over Moses, and he felt that life was unfair. He hadn't asked for this. This was more than he had bargained for. The Lord had placed him in this position, and he now felt totally inadequate to perform his responsibilities. I know just what he was feeling, and you probably do too.

But this is all part of our spiritual battle. The objective of the enemy is to attack us with a spirit of depression and cause us to want to die. Then he won't have to use anyone else to kill us. We'll do it ourselves. What causes this? And how can we avoid it?

One of my respected mentors said something to me several years ago that really got my attention. He said, "Bishop, I need to tell you something. Because you're so serious about your relationship with God and about the ministry He has given you, the devil knows that he can never stop you by making you lazy and unproductive. He knows that he can't get you sitting down, so he'll try to get you while you're working yourself to death." This is something, I have found, that we all need to guard against.

Moses was simply exhausted, and his responsibility was suddenly more than he could bear. This burden was too heavy, and he was no longer willing, or able, to bear it. "Just let me die," he prayed. "Take me. Kill me." It's hard to imagine, but it happened.

God had called and anointed Moses to lead His people into the Promised Land, and now he was being attacked in this horrible way. You can expect some similar attacks to come to your life because of your high calling in God.

Elijah Was Depressed

And Ahab told Jezebel all that Elijah had done, also how he had executed all the prophets with the sword. Then Jezebel sent a messenger to Elijah, saying, "So let the gods do to me, and more also, if I do not make your life as the life of one of them by tomorrow about this time." And when he saw that, he arose and ran for his life, and went to Beersheba, which belongs to Judah, and left his servant there. But he himself went a day's journey into the wilderness, and came and sat down under a broom tree [a juniper tree]. And he prayed that he might die, and he said,

Learning to Battle Depression

"It is enough! Now, Lord, take my life, for I am no better than my fathers!"

1 Kings 19:1–4

Was this the great prophet of God? Was this the same man who had just called down fire out of heaven? Was this the man whom God had utilized to work miracles? Was this the real Elijah? Look at him now. When he received the word that Jezebel was coming to kill him, he tucked his tail between his legs like a scared dog and ran for his life.

Now we find him sitting under a juniper tree praying that he would die. "This is enough, Lord," he was saying. "Take my life." That's about as hopeless as you can get.

Moses had been God's servant, and it happened to him. Now Elijah, God's prophet, was so depressed that he wanted to die.

"It's enough."

"This is too much. I can't handle it."

So here it is again. Many of us experience these or similar emotions because of the things that happen to us on our jobs, in our personal lives, at church, with our money, with our children, or with other family members. At the time, they seem absolutely overwhelming, and we cry out, "Lord, this is just too much for me."

When any of us prays to die, it's a sure sign of depression. As I have said, wanting to die before we have fulfilled our destinies on earth is not normal, and it certainly isn't inspired by God. So we know where these thoughts come from.

Jonah Was Depressed

But it displeased Jonah exceedingly, and he became angry. So he prayed to the Lord, and said, "Ah, Lord, was not this what I said when I was still in my country? Therefore I fled previously to Tarshish; for I know that You are a gracious and merciful God, slow to anger and abundant in lovingkindness, One who relents from doing harm. Therefore now, O LORD, please take my life from me, for it is better for me to die than to live!"

Jonah 4:1–3

Most of us have known the story of Jonah since childhood. God told him to go to Nineveh, but he didn't want to go, so he boarded a ship going in the opposite direction. The next thing he knew, he found himself in the belly of the whale, crying out and asking God for another chance. God gave him that second chance by allowing the fish to spit him out on dry land.

Jonah repented, and then he went on and did what God had called him to do. It would have been better, of course, if he had just done it in the first place, but he got it done anyway. Most of us can't criticize Jonah because we know what it's like to take the long road to Nineveh. We've done it ourselves—some of us many times.

Now, after all of that, a serious depression has settled over the prophet. How interesting.

My Own Experience with Depression

Personally, I would not be able to teach God's Word with the effectiveness I do if I had not gone through some things in my personal life. (And what you're currently experiencing can ultimately be of benefit to you too.) I know what it's like to be depressed, and, like many, I didn't even know how depressed I was. It got so bad that I didn't want to leave the house and I didn't want to see anyone. I just sat there thinking, *World, leave me alone.* But, after a while, I realized that I couldn't go on living like that.

We, however, are too blessed to be stressed. There's too much work waiting for us to do. We have to rise up and tell the devil, "Get this spirit off of me. The joy of the Lord is my strength!"

When people try you and convict you without any evidence, when people lie about you and forget all the good things you've ever done, that's the time the enemy will attack your mind. And he knows how to add insult to injury and to heap trouble on you. He's a master at it.

I was deeply depressed one day, and I bumped into a brother in the bank. He said, "Bishop, I'm praying for you." He couldn't have known how powerful those words were to me at the moment.

I said, "Thank you, sir. Thank you. Thank you."

I went to McDonald's one day so depressed that I didn't want to go inside for fear that I would meet someone I knew and have to talk to the person. I pulled up at the drive-thru order area, but I didn't even want to speak with the woman who was taking the orders. Somehow I felt that she ought to know what I wanted.

I quickly realized that this was impossible, so I would have to order. I did, and when I pulled through to the other window to pay, someone I knew was inside looking out at me. "Bishop," he said, "I'm praying for you!" I felt about like Elijah at that moment. I just wanted to die, and only my faith in God sustained me.

So becoming depressed doesn't mean that you're not saved or that you don't know the Lord. It doesn't mean that you're not filled with the Holy Ghost and speak in tongues. I am witness to this fact. Despite all of these blessings in your life, your depression can be very real.

For me it was worse. As the pastor of a large congregation, I was expected to always be up, to always have the victory. I had to go onto the platform and teach my people how to fight depression—

when I was battling it myself. I had to stand up and blow the trumpet for them, telling them that it was time to march, when I felt like collapsing myself.

Any depression is a serious thing. It's not to be played with or minimized. And if great men like these, who had a one-on-one, personal relationship with God, could suffer it, so can you. If they were so overwhelmed and so burdened that they could see no way out, you could experience this too. If they just wanted to die, you might have the same desire at some point. If they felt wretched and miserable enough to ask God to take their lives, you need to learn from their experiences.

The spirit of depression can attach itself to your mind and your psyche and become a part of you. When it happens, your nerves are bad, you're short-tempered, and absolutely everything ticks you off.

Could it be that, like others and like myself, some of you are depressed and don't even know it? Could it be that you've been down so long that you've decided that this is the way life is supposed to be? If so, a stronghold has developed in your mind. A negative mind-set is dominating you and making you think that your situation is hopeless, unchangeable.

If you are feeling helpless and hopeless and are experiencing a deep sadness, I have some good news for you. That spirit of depression can be put under your feet this very day.

Physical Exhaustion Leads to Depression

It is important for us to know what opens the door to depression, so that we can avoid it. There are many things that lead to depression, but several important ones come to mind first. I am compelled to mention them because prevention is always better than cure. If you're not already depressed, let God give you the understanding of what will protect you when depression does come knocking at your door. Then you'll recognize him for what he is, and you can send him away quickly.

The first thing that can lead to depression is physical exhaustion. This opens a huge door to the enemy, and far too many of us are not getting enough rest these days. There are too many responsibilities in modern life—and far too much entertainment—and our rest suffers as a consequence.

Many complain that even when they do go to sleep, they're not resting well. When they wake up in the morning, they feel just as tired as they did when they went to bed. This is part of our spiritual warfare. For many of us, our private lives are so out of order that they give us no rest.

God has constructed each day with a purpose in mind. He has given us just twenty-four hours for each day, and that breaks down roughly into three equal parts—eight hours of sleep, eight hours of work, and eight hours of recreation.

Most of us don't get nearly enough sleep and many don't get enough recreation. For many Christians, recreation is almost a dirty word. But recreation means re-creation. It is to be a time of restoration. Stop working yourself to death.

I have noticed through the years that some of the people I minister to in churches and conferences are so physically exhausted that once they sit down, they can't stay awake.

They try everything possible to keep themselves alert. They shake themselves and change positions often. But they just can't fight the sleep that overcomes them. Their bodies are sleep deprived. Even when they are physically awake, their minds are asleep.

This also can be partly a result of our spiritual battle. No sooner do we get to church than we begin to feel sleepy. No sooner do we get on our knees to pray than we begin to feel sleepy. We can then go home and watch television until all hours of the night, but it's hard for us to stay alert throughout a forty-five minute sermon. This shows that it's part of a spiritual battle.

If you don't believe it, notice that as soon as church is over, you suddenly feel awake. So if you find you can't sleep some night, a good remedy might be to get down on your knees and start praying. That will work better than a sleeping pill.

The devil doesn't want you spending time with God. He doesn't want you talking to God. He doesn't want life coming to your spirit. So he sends drowsiness to you.

Rebuke those spirits of sleepiness in the name of Jesus. What God wants to do in us is too important to sleep through it. We need God to speak to us, and we must be alert to hear His voice.

Moses was physically "worn out," and that led to his depression. Elijah was hungry because he had gone without food for a long period of time, and on top of that, he was also physically exhausted because he had just finished a thirty-mile cross-country run. It was when he was so exhausted that he had to stop and sit down under a tree to rest that the desire to die came to him.

Jonah was also physically exhausted. He'd had a "whalehouse" for a jailhouse and then had just preached a citywide revival in a place about the size of Philadelphia. (We're told that ancient Nineveh had more than a million inhabitants.) I'm sure that when Jonah had finished preaching, some people wanted prayer, and he probably laid his hands on thousands of people.

Jonah was an evangelist, but they didn't have nice hotels in his day or nice cars that he could use to transport himself from place to place. There was also no convenient public transportation. It was a rough life, and it tired him dramatically.

Each of these men, then, was physically exhausted, and when physical exhaustion sets in to your body, it opens the door for depression.

The legendary coach of the Green Bay Packers, the late Vince Lombardi, once said, "Fatigue makes cowards of us all." It doesn't matter how strong we are—physically, mentally, emotionally, or spiritually—when fatigue sets in, we all bow to it. Sometimes we get so tired that we seem incapable of holding on to life. This is a dangerous state to be in, and it should be avoided at all costs.

It's dangerous to drive when you're tired. You make mistakes and cause accidents. It's absolutely crazy for children and young people to go to school tired. They can never do their best in that condition.

And it's terrible when men and women go to work tired. When you walk into your workplace and someone says, "Good morning," too often your response is, "What's so good about it?" That shows that you're too tired, and you need some rest.

When was the last time you took a break and got away from everything just to relax and rest? When was the last time you had a day just for pampering yourself? When was the last time you broke away from everything just to give your body a much needed rest?

We simply must find time for rest, and we must find time for recreation. Go rent a good movie, then sit down and eat some popcorn and relax. That may not sound very spiritual to some, but it's important nevertheless.

Most of us don't have enough time for serious prayer and fasting. That also can help to rest our spirits and our bodies. Then we can be more victorious against demon spirits.

Psychological Turmoil Leads to Depression

Another thing that can lead to depression is psychological turmoil. In the common vernacular, that means "stuff messing with your mind." When you're under attack in your mind, you begin to view the events of life differently—from the wrong angle. Suddenly, you can't find any good in it. As we were growing up, we often heard the phrase, "An idle mind is the devil's workshop." He loves it, and he attacks our minds, causing psychological turmoil.

Every one of these three men—Moses, Elijah, and Jonah—was not only physically exhausted, but was also under psychological attack, and that gave the enemy his opening. Elijah didn't really want to die. If he had wanted to die, he surely wouldn't have run from Jezebel. He would have stayed right there and let her catch him.

He didn't really want to die. He just said that because he was under so much stress. Jezebel's threats were almost worse than the real thing.

There's nothing wrong with encountering trouble in life. All of us will. It *is* wrong, however, to allow our troubles to get the best of us. That's when we get in trouble.

Depression often comes to us when something we love and value very much is threatened or taken from us. It could be possessions or it could be a loved one. Many of those who lose a loved one are still depressed about it many years later.

When anything like this happens, we suddenly find ourselves in positions we didn't ask to be in. But God has promised that everything is for our good, so we can relax and not worry. He has our welfare in mind in everything that He does.

Trust Him—even when you can't see Him. Trust Him—even when you don't understand what He's doing. He will never put more upon you than you are able to bear. Just when, as we say, you're about to "lose it," He'll step in and undertake for you.

Learning to Battle Depression

When you say to God, "I can't take anymore," and He says, "Yes, you can," trust Him that He knows how much you can bear. When you feel that you're on the verge of collapse, don't worry. He'll reach down, pick you up, turn you around, and give you deliverance. That's why we praise Him.

God has been too good to me for me to walk around depressed, and, as the Scriptures declare, *"Therefore if the Son makes you free, you shall be free indeed"* (John 8:36).

Believe me, when I say that you're too blessed to be stressed and that God hasn't brought you this far to leave you now. You can't die now because there are too many promises God has made to you that haven't yet come to pass. And if God said a thing, He will to do it. He simply cannot fail in this regard.

Our text verse said, *"Though we walk in the flesh, we do not war according to the flesh."* When you're fighting the devil, you can't use a scud missile, a nine-millimeter pistol, or an M-16 rifle. But God has given you a powerful weapon, and that weapon is praise.

Accept God's will and praise Him for what He's doing, for He knows what's best for you. If you will just let Him have His way, He will fix things.

Some of you have been so depressed that you felt the weight of the world on your shoulders, but God is going to free you and let you feel as light as a feather. That heavy weight is coming off.

This thing is all about a spiritual battle, and life is too short for you not to be happy. Don't walk around depressed, oppressed, and worried about situations you can do nothing about.

Spiritual Weakness Leads to Depression

A third thing that leads to depression is spiritual weakness. When you're weak spiritually, when you don't know the Word of

God, the enemy doesn't have to put much effort into attacking you in order to destroy you. He is a master strategist, and he knows exactly when to move in and when to attack you with a fit of despondency that can take you out.

As a Christian, you can easily get into trouble spiritually when you're in trouble physically and psychologically. The enemy knows that if he can get you off balance physically, and if he can get you off balance psychologically, he won't have to do much to get you off balance spiritually as well.

The only reason he has been able to attack so many Christians successfully with a spirit of depression is that their lives are out of balance spiritually, mentally, emotionally, and psychologically. When you face some difficulty, that's when the devil will move in.

As we have seen, even great men of God can be spiritually run down. Why did Moses, Elijah, and Jonah get in trouble? It was because they had taken their eyes off the Lord and put them on people, on themselves, or on their circumstances. This is the objective of the devil. He wants you to gaze at your problems and just occasionally glance at God. With many of us, we are gazing at what we should be glancing at, and we're glancing at what we should be gazing at—because God is bigger than any of our problems.

Satan was able to attack these anointed men of God because he broke their focus, and if he can break your focus—causing you to put your eyes on people, self, or circumstances—you, like any other Christian, can be prone to depression.

The anointing of God is present to set you free. The fact that you've been depressed or attacked by a spirit of depression, as I have shown, has absolutely nothing to do with the thought that you're not saved, you don't love the Lord, or you're not in His will. Put these lies behind you once and for all.

Learning to Battle Depression

If you are battling with a spirit of depression, this word is for you. It doesn't matter if you're young or old, you have to get your eyes off of people, off yourself, and off your circumstances, and you have to look to Him who is anointed to deliver you.

Other Causes of Depression

Depression is often the result of our unwillingness to fully obey God. It comes when He asks us to accept what, in our eyes, is unacceptable, and we feel incapable of doing it. The secret of relief is to say, as Jesus did, "Lord, not my will, but Thy will be done." Why is it that we cannot just step back and say, "God, You know what's best for me, and if You have me going through this, then there must be a reason for it. I don't understand it, but I'm willing to trust You and be content."

Accept His will; you can't do anything about it anyway. Stop losing sleep over the situations of life. Stop killing yourself with worry. Stop letting your blood pressure soar. Just accept the will of God.

When you finally accept His will, you will say, "Lord, this doesn't meet my approval, but who am I to complain? You are God, so I yield to You."

Stop worrying yourself to death about every little detail of life. If you can't do anything about a certain circumstance, then just accept it and rest in God. He let it happen, so stop fretting yourself about it.

The spirit of depression has to go, as we allow God to be God. He knows what He's doing, and if He has allowed something to happen, then that's His business.

LIVING THE DREAM

Depression Can Lead to Suicide

Every one of us goes through tests and trials, but we can never allow our tests and trials to get the best of us. You may wonder if anyone else can really understand what you're going through, and maybe no one can. But there is One who knows. Tell Him all about it, and He will help you.

You must be set free from your depression, since depression can lead to suicide. Many of those who are depressed become so hopeless and so helpless and so sad that their whole attitude toward life changes. Suddenly, they are just wandering through life, with no real zest for living. Their days are filled with activity, but they are seeing no results. Life suddenly seems to them like a treadmill. They're perspiring, but they're not getting anywhere. Their minds are suddenly filled with negatives, and they focus on the worst of them.

This is a very dangerous place to be, but the Lord wants to set you free. Freedom is yours. God has too much in store for you, too many places for you to go, and too many things for you to do.

What is it about you that so intimidates the devil? Why is it that he started attacking you when you were just a small child? Could he see already that you were destined for great things in God?

Many, who haven't gone through half of what you've gone through, didn't make it. They lost their minds. But God has preserved you. Right now, I apply the blood of the Lamb over your life. I declare and decree that no weapon that has been formed against you will prosper. Let every trace of depression be gone from your life right now.

When you obtain deliverance from depression, you move toward your goal of *Living the Dream*.

Chapter Eight

LEARNING TO
OVERCOME REJECTION

He is despised and rejected by men. A Man of sorrows and acquainted with grief. And we hid, as it were, our faces from Him; He was despised, and we did not esteem Him. Surely He has borne our griefs and carried our sorrows; yet we esteemed Him stricken, smitten by God, and afflicted. But He was wounded for our transgressions, He was bruised for our iniquities; the chastisement for our peace was upon Him, and by His stripes we are healed.

Isaiah 53:3–5

This passage from Isaiah 53 is the most popular prophecy of the crucifixion found in the Bible. Both Matthew and Peter quoted from it years later, for God had used the prophet to foretell with great clarity exactly what our Lord and Savior would go through as He hung dying on that hated and hideous instrument of torture called the cross.

What makes this text so powerful is that God used Isaiah to foretell these events eight centuries before Jesus even came on the scene. This has amazed people now for centuries.

Isaiah foretold that Jesus, our Savior, would be *"despised and rejected by men,"* and since we know that *"a servant is not greater than his master"* (John 15:20), this means that you and I should expect to experience the same thing Jesus went through. Experiencing rejection is not intended to break us but to strengthen us so that we can fulfill our purpose in life. As unwelcoming as this statement may be, rejection is something that most of us know about firsthand.

This message is not for the mediocre churchgoer, but for those who want to bring the outward person into line with the inner reality. People are not just what they appear to be on the outside. Inwardly, there's a lot more going on.

It's just as important to have our inner wounds healed as it is to have our outer, or physical, wounds healed. If a person receives a cut on his hand, he is quick to cleanse that wound and to put something over it to protect it while it heals. We do this because we've learned that there's always the possibility of a wound becoming infected. And if infection is allowed to set it, it greatly complicates the injury and prolongs the healing process.

This possibility of complication also applies to our inner wounds. Still, when many of us incur inner wounds, we never seem to get around to cleansing them. When an inner wound is experienced, it must be immediately cleansed by applying forgiveness. This is powerful medicine. Forgiveness is a spiritual antiseptic.

Learning to Overcome Rejection

Judge not, and you shall not be judged. Condemn not, and you shall not be condemned. Forgive, and you will be forgiven.

Luke 6:37

If you are wounded inwardly, and you fail to apply the spiritual antiseptic of forgiveness, an unclean spirit (which is a spiritual germ) may gain entrance into the wound and cause a spiritual infection. So when anyone is wounded by rejection, he must quickly forgive the offending party.

There are many people in the body of Christ who are very gifted, but they have never become as effective as they might have been because they are spiritually infected. That's why, when you rub them the wrong way, their response shocks you. You never imagined that a person who looked so loving and kind could turn into someone very different, and so quickly.

How did Jesus react when He was wounded and rejected by men? How did He respond? The answer is that while He was dying from the wounds they had inflicted on Him, He prayed, *"Father, forgive them"* (Luke 23:34).

How many know that a dying man wants to reserve his last breaths for important things? So there was nothing more important in Jesus' heart than forgiving those who had wounded Him. *"They do not know what they do,"* He prayed (Luke 23:34).

Jesus, although He had been rejected, did not react angrily. This, of course, is not normal. There's something in all of us that rises up when we're wronged. The desire for revenge is a strong one. We love to say to people, "You barked up the wrong tree this time; you 'messed with' the wrong person this time." Even as Christians, we don't want people to think that we're weak or that they can walk all over us. Whether we say something to them or not, we often carry a deep wound within.

115

That's just what the devil wants. He loves it when we're wounded and we neglect to cleanse the wound. He wants that wound to lie open, so he will send along a few more people to agitate it once in a while.

Our greatest hurts are often not caused by the "people of the world," but by the people of the church. They smile in your face, then they stab you in the back. That hurts, but it's time to get over it—in the name of Jesus.

Rejection is a very real emotion, and it leaves many people severely damaged. Physical infirmities often emerge out of the emotional stress caused by rejection, and that's just an indication of how very serious these wounds can be.

Jesus Was Rejected in Nazareth

Toward the beginning of His earthly ministry, Jesus went into the synagogue in His hometown and read the scripture text for the day:

And He was handed the book of the prophet Isaiah. And when He had opened the book, He found the place where it was written: "The Spirit of the LORD is upon Me, because He has anointed Me to preach the gospel to the poor; He has sent Me to heal the brokenhearted, to proclaim liberty to the captives and recovery of sight to the blind, to set at liberty those who are oppressed [bruised, KJV]; to proclaim the acceptable year of the LORD."

Luke 4:17–19

Jesus had come back to Nazareth to reveal His destiny, His purpose; He came to show His people what His ministry was to be. And He found the words to describe it in Isaiah. The Spirit of the Lord, He said, had come upon Him and anointed Him for specific purposes. He was anointed to preach the Gospel, the Good News, to the poor.

But there was more. He was also sent *"to heal the brokenhearted."* This was the first declared purpose for Jesus' coming and for the preaching of the Gospel. He was also sent *"to set at liberty them that are bruised"* (KJV).

Most of us understand brokenheartedness well. It is the result of an inner wound, and those who have been brokenhearted and bruised need deliverance and healing. This is a ministry that is much in need in the body of Christ today. People of every stripe—even those with titles, positions, and prestige—often need deliverance. Jesus came for this express purpose.

I would go so far as to say that most of the people I meet need healing in this regard. Just about every Christian needs this kind of deliverance. Some people need to be healed physically, and what we have done in the body of Christ is to give greater attention to those physical needs. This is wrong, for we too seldom deal with the person who looks good on the outside, and may even be helping around the altar or serving the church in some other way, but who desperately needs deliverance in his inner man.

As Jesus launched His ministry, they brought to Him people from all walks of life who were afflicted with every sort of malady—physical and emotional alike—and *"He healed them"* (Matthew 4:24). So His will is to heal us inside, just as He does the outside.

Although rejection is one of the most common wounds we can suffer, it is perhaps the most neglected. The seeds of rejection often lie dormant for years before bringing forth a deadly harvest. How sad that no one has taught us how to disinfect our wounds so that they do not endanger our destinies!

With many, wounds are the result of a lover who has used them in their youth and then abandoned them, leaving a sore wound. When the wounded person finally finds their life mate, they have probably gone through several of these woundings, compounding other wounds received in childhood, and are thus damaged goods, carrying infection in their spirits.

Rejection doesn't have to be overt. It can result from the denial of love. When a person is loved, he is approved and accepted. But when he is rejected, he is disapproved and refused.

Too often we have been taught that when it hurts we should not admit it; we should just get over it and move on. Many do move on, but they never get over it.

Jesus was despised and rejected, and some of us have been through a whole cycle of rejection. It seems to follow us everywhere we go—even through our adult years.

Some may think that they have never suffered rejection and imagine that this part of the book is for others. But just what is rejection? Here are some synonyms of *rejection*: refusal, denial, being turned down, rebuffed, given the cold shoulder, slighted, ignored, neglected, taken for granted, avoided, disapproved. When you have experienced any of these things, there is a self-defense mechanism on the inside of you that kicks in and raises a wall.

When that wall goes up, you move on to the next stage of your life, but if what triggered that wall is not dealt with, there may be permanent damage. Just because you transfer to another church doesn't mean that the hurt is over. Just because you move to another city doesn't mean that the hurt is over. Just because you get a new husband or a new wife doesn't mean that the hurt is over. At some point, you have to deal with what is on the inside of you.

Some of us have moved on physically, but mentally and emotionally, the person who rejected us still keeps us on an invisible chain. This is the reason we need to be careful about forming casual relationships with people of the opposite sex. The person you think you are attracted to may have many chains around his or her neck already.

If you're wondering why a friend of your is up and down, in and out, and has no consistency, it could be that there's a serious wound on the inside that has never been cleaned out. Unless your friend can be set free, he or she may never become stable or reliable.

Many of us have hurts so tender that when we hear someone's name or see his or her face, we're plunged into a cauldron of emotions. God wants to heal us of all past wounds so that when we hear the names and see the faces of those who have hurt us, there is no reaction at all. Jesus was anointed to heal broken hearts, and He does it well.

Every Creature Alive Requires Love

Each of us requires love. This is not just something that we desire. We need it. Love is necessary for the development of a healthy self-life. Love is to us what sunshine and water are to a flower. They cause the flower to grow and develop.

Anyone who believes that he does not require love from others is deceived. Some say, "I don't need anybody to love me," but that's not true.

"I don't care. I don't have anybody, I'm not looking for anybody, and I don't even want anybody." It may sound good, but it's not true. That is hurt speaking. What that person is really saying is, "Lord, please send me somebody who will put his or her arms around me and love me." It doesn't matter how much you love God. Every now and then you need someone other than Jesus to hold you.

LIVING THE DREAM

Some say, "I'm so thankful that I can live in the arms of Jesus." That's fine, but sometimes you also long for some physical arms around you. Jesus speaks to me, and He tells me of His love, but sometimes I need somebody else to whisper sweet nothings in my ear and to let me know that my existence is significant.

Even animals respond to love. Humane societies hire people who love animals because the animals respond to this show of affection. It keeps them healthier. They eat better and are better adjusted when they're treated with kindness. If that's true of dogs, how much more so of humans?

Some children are birthed through rejection. We may not realize how the mother's attitude affects them, but it does. Sometimes a child was not planned, and, therefore, is not welcome. The mother may go on and have the child, but she's not happy about it.

Her attitude also may have something to do with issues she has with the child's father, and suddenly loving her own child becomes a challenge. Wounds like these are not easy for a child to cast off, and they can remain inside for many years.

When a person is wounded internally, abnormalities often develop in their character, and they become unstable. As a pastor, I find that understanding this helps me to love some people despite their peculiarities. I know that it's often not their fault. When I see good people fluctuating in their attitudes and behavior, I'm able to look beyond their actions and see an inner problem caused by something they suffered years before.

Many of us never really come to God until we're torn apart inwardly, and so even those of us who are saved have had some unstable behavior, some fluctuating attitudes, in our past. I know people who are one way on Sunday, when they smile and embrace and greet me, and on some other day of the week they are completely different people. It seems as though I don't even know them.

I never take this personally because it's my job, as a prophet of God, to uproot and to tear down. God has put me in the lives of some people to help make some of their crooked ways straight. They don't always love me, since I'm constantly challenging them to move on to the next level, but I understand that. Every day I make sure that I put forth the greatest effort possible to be understanding of the people around me.

The Fear of Rejection

When a wound of rejection is introduced into a person's life, two parallel problems begin to emerge. This can happen, and often does, very early in life either because our father is not there for us or because he gave us his word and never kept it. The first problem that emerges is fear of rejection.

When a person has been wounded, he recoils from the prospect of further wounding. He's been hurt once, and now he walks around with a chip on his shoulder. This is the person who says, "Who can I trust? I don't trust anybody."

Others may not voice their mistrust, but inwardly they are saying, "Will I be hurt again by those who made me suffer? And will other people also inflict similar wounds on me? He looks like a good man, but will he be just like the other one?"

This fear can prevent a person from developing a good relationship. A woman may be thinking, *He may make me cry, but I'll only cry with one eye, since with the other I'll be watching him the whole time.*

Even when God places people into our lives, we find that we cannot trust them. Everyone is suddenly suspect. We mean well by this, for we intend to avoid further hurts, but the result is the stifling of healthy relationships. We're constantly second-guessing the people around us.

Psychologists call this paranoia. One minute we're singing and shouting, smiling and giving people high fives, and the next moment we're suddenly very different.

As the pattern of mistrust and suspicion grows, fears eventually develop that others are plotting against us. We become convinced that certain people have singled us out as a target for persecution. When this happens, we can no longer do what God has called us to do because we don't trust the very people He has given us to work with. And how can we maximize our potential if we don't trust any of the people God has put in place to help us?

The devil delights in knowing that our feelings of rejection have never been dealt with. That gives him firm ground to stand on. Patiently he waits for his opportunity to send yet another person into our lives to hurt us. Then he sends another and another. His goal is to ultimately finish us off, and it's all done through the fear of rejection.

Many of us have visions and dreams on the inside of us, and God has told us to do something great, but we're not doing it because we're afraid to fail. "What if I fail?" we say. But what if you don't?

We feel more secure being in the boat where it's much safer, but as long as we stay in the boat, we can never walk on water. We would never try to walk on water. After all, what would happen if we sank? There's that old fear of rejection showing its ugly head again and keeping us from God's very best for our lives.

Self-Rejection

The second parallel problem that emerges from uncleansed wounds is self-rejection. When any of us has suffered the wound of rejection, the enemy tries to make us feel that it was our own fault. We are to blame, so we begin to hate ourselves.

We begin to think, *If I could just be different,* or *if I could just be like someone else, maybe I could accomplish something in life. Maybe then I would be loved and appreciated.* When this happens, we try to actually become like someone else whom we admire, mimicking him or her in every way we can. Some actually try to live someone else's life. This delights the devil. As we have seen, he knows that if we can't learn to love ourselves, we'll never be able to fully love others.

When we reject the self that God has created, we open ourselves to alternate personalities, any of which could be demonically inspired. Whenever we begin acting like someone else, it can be very dangerous. What we're really saying to God is, "You made a mistake when You made me. You should have made me like that other person. So now, since I can't be him, I'll try to at least act like him or dress like him."

Self-rejection is the door through which multiple personality disorders and schizophrenia enter. Doctors may diagnose it as little more than a chemical imbalance, but it's much more than that. It's a spiritual problem, and one that often can be traced all the way back to childhood or adolescence.

A person who has been wounded often lacks the ability to relate well to others. They are very judgmental and unforgiving. Far too many Christians are gifted and glamorous on the outside, but inside they are severely damaged by rejection.

If you're like that, let the Holy Spirit touch you. Let Him deal with you. Receive His deliverance, and then *"do not be entangled again with a yoke of bondage"* (Galatians 5:1). It doesn't matter what people have done to you; the Lord is saying, "Get over it." No one is worth your blessings being cut off.

You've been rejected. So what? Jesus was rejected too.

You've been misused and abused. So what? Jesus was misused and abused too.

You've been taken advantage of. So what? Jesus was taken advantage of too.

I hear the Lord saying, "Go on to be who I called you to be. Go on to do what I called you to do. Don't let the failures of others hinder your destiny."

Stop second-guessing everyone around you. Begin to trust them, and begin to trust yourself. And, whatever you do, don't worry about the people who have done you harm. God will deal with them. We often quote the scripture that says, *"Do not touch My anointed ones, and do My prophets no harm"* (1 Chronicles 16:22). Those *"anointed ones"* are not all men of the cloth. That's speaking about you too. You are the anointed of God.

God knows how to deal with your enemies. Hear what He says:

"Therefore all those who devour you shall be devoured; and all your adversaries, every one of them, shall go into captivity; those who plunder you shall become plunder, and all who prey upon you I will make a prey. For I will restore health to you and heal you of your wounds," says the LORD, "because they called you an outcast...."

Jeremiah 30:16–17

God is about to show your enemies that they can't oppose you and prosper because you are His child. At the same time, you should be glad that you were kicked out of certain circles. God never intended for you to run with the turkeys. You're an eagle, and there's greatness on the inside of you. Let it come out. If God is for you, who can be against you?

Learning to Overcome Rejection

Start thanking God for your enemies. Thank Him for those who kicked you around and hurt you. From this day forth, you will never feel rejected again, simply because Jesus loves you so much.

Praise God because you've been an outcast. Thank Him because you don't fit in with the crowd. Thank Him because you've been misunderstood. Give Him praise because people think you're crazy. They have accused you of having a "holier-than-thou" attitude. That's fine.

God will call to account those who have done you harm. Leave them in His hands. Men can't stop you. No one can hold you back. God is on your side. Therefore, you must never feel rejection again.

Get delivered from the fear of rejection. Get delivered from self-rejection. I speak deliverance into your life now, in the name of the Lord Jesus Christ. Right now, I come against every mental attack: oppression, depression, and rejection. I rebuke you now, in the name of Jesus. Satan, loose God's people and let them go free, in Jesus' name.

As you are healed of rejection, you are taking one more giant step toward *Living the Dream.*

LIVING THE DREAM

Chapter Nine

LEARNING TO DEAL WITH TEMPTATION

Blessed is the man who endures temptation; for when he has been approved, he will receive the crown of life which the Lord has promised to those who love Him. Let no one say when he is tempted, "I am tempted by God"; for God cannot be tempted by evil, nor does He Himself tempt anyone. But each one is tempted when he is drawn away by his own desires and enticed. Then, when desire has conceived, it gives birth to sin; and sin, when it is full-grown, brings forth death. Do not be deceived, my beloved brethren.

James 1:12–16

As a spiritual father and pastor, I'm responsible to my people, but I'm certainly not responsible for them. God holds each and every one of us responsible for the revelation He entrusts to us. The Bible says,

Therefore, to him who knows to do good and does not do it, to him it is sin.

James 4:17

"To him it is sin," not to anyone else. Therefore we all need to learn to deal with the temptations that come to us.

Dietrich Bonhoeffer was a very famous and respected German theologian whose life was brought to an early end by Adolph Hitler (he was executed by Hitler when he was just thirty-nine years old). I once read something he wrote about temptation, and I found it very compelling. Bonhoeffer talked about how even Christians can fall to temptation. What he said was, in effect, that when temptation comes, and when our minds have been made up that we're going to go ahead and entertain the temptation, at that point, God is very unreal to us. That's how the enemy is able to capitalize on the fact. It's not that we hate God; it's that we have forgotten Him for the moment.

Not a single person on earth has not faced temptation. That includes Jesus Christ. But only Jesus has ever faced temptation and not given in to it.

All of us are tempted, and unless we can learn to understand temptation and deal with it, we are destined to live defeated lives. The consequences of sin are serious, and the fact that Christians go on sinning is tragic.

Unfortunately, temptation is an inevitable fact of life. You can't escape it. Even Jesus was tempted.

For we do not have a High Priest who cannot sympathize with our weaknesses, but was in all points tempted as we are, yet without sin.

Hebrews 4:15

Learning to Deal with Temptation

Jesus is surely the only person who has never yielded to sin, but His strength in resisting gives us hope that we can too—by His power.

James spoke of the man who *"endures temptation"* and said that he would be *"blessed."* He will be *"tried"* (KJV), James showed, and when he has endured, he *"will receive the crown of life which the Lord has promised to those who love Him."*

Temptation Explained

James also made it very clear that temptation does not originate with God. He does not tempt anyone. So, when some evil comes before you, God is not just trying to see what you will do. He, being omniscient, already knows what you will do before any temptation comes. There are times when you're not sure how you will respond, but God already knows. So He doesn't need to merely test us in this way.

Verse 14 is very important. Each of us is tempted when we are drawn away by our own desires. This is why we have been tempted and will be tempted, and it is why, if some of us are man or woman enough to admit it, we have given in to temptation at some point. (Of course, there were consequences of that failure to resist.) The true nature of temptation will become more apparent as we discuss several types of temptation.

So, although Satan is the source of all temptation, no one can blame him for sinful deeds or even for its roots. The roots of the sinful deed lies within the individual. Satan is the agent who comes to offer a means of bringing into manifestation what's already on the inside of men and women. Therefore if there's nothing on the inside, then he has nothing to work with. If there is no desire, he eventually moves on.

Satan may be the external force behind temptation, but he's not the one to be blamed. He is what he is, and he'll never change. Again, the root of every sinful deed lies within the individual. Jesus spoke at length about this subject (see Mark 7:1–23).

It's also very interesting to realize that we all are tempted by very different things. You can sit right next to someone in church and never know what tempts him. "Your thing" may not be "my thing," and "my thing" may not be "their thing," but we all have "a thing." Something that you and I don't give a second thought to may become a stronghold for others, and something they would never consider may be very tempting to you. The enemy places us under surveillance to find out what we like and what will tempt us.

When temptation shows its ugly head, its appearance is often very different. If we can learn the various faces of temptation, it can help us to resist. And when we have learned to resist a certain temptation, that same temptation rarely comes to us again. The ones we yield to come to us over and over again, since Satan knows well our particular area of weakness.

Material Temptation

The first type of temptation I want to discuss is something I call material temptation. Many people struggle with this type of temptation. Just what is material temptation? It's a lust for things. When people are tempted in this way, their whole thought life is consumed with how to acquire more "stuff." This temptation can be as big as a house or as a small as a ring. It doesn't always have to be for something big. It can be as bright as a brand-new car or as dusty as an old antique.

But if there is no desire within, then there is no temptation. If you don't desire things, then the devil can't tempt you with them.

Learning to Deal with Temptation

When there is an internal desire, that gives the enemy a door, and we consequently have a greater proclivity toward this particular sin. If the desire isn't there, the devil could try to tempt us with material things all he wanted, and it wouldn't faze us.

Let me give an example, something we all can relate to. When it comes offering time, certain Christians struggle with the command to tithe, and they often fail. These same people struggle financially month after month and year after year and are never blessed, although in every other way they seem to love God with their whole hearts. This one test seems to be difficult for them, and they fail it—miserably. I'm afraid that this indicates a desire in their hearts for more money, for if that desire was not there, they wouldn't struggle with the temptation to keep what belongs to God.

The devil's intention is clear when he tempts men and women in this way. He hopes to keep them in such tight financial straits that they cannot give like they want to, and they will always need more. This only further complicates their plight, tempting them to hold on to what they already have. If all of your bills are already paid and you have so much money that you don't know what to do with, tithing might be much easier. For those who constantly struggle, it is sometimes very difficult.

The devil tells people, rich and poor alike, that it's foolish to give ten percent of their money to God, but we know that it is correct and beneficial to give that much—and more. But, when a person is in constant need for his or her own daily necessities, tithing becomes difficult to do (and, in fact, a surprising percentage of Christians do not tithe).

There are many others ways in which material temptation affects us, but this gives us a good idea of its power.

Personal Temptation

The second face that temptation can wear is something I call personal temptation. What's the difference between material temptation and personal temptation? With material temptation, we lust for things, but with personal temptation, we lust for a name, for authority, for power, or for control over others. For some individuals, this is their struggle, and they are consumed by it.

People who have this problem would die for a certain title. It means everything to them, and they would do almost anything to attain it.

There is nothing wrong with having ambition, nothing wrong with having goals, and nothing wrong with not being satisfied with where you are today. The key is to be content where you are and still want more at the same time.

It's not wrong to be ambitious, but it *is* wrong to feel that you deserve a title or a certain authority or to begin to compare yourself with others who have titles or authority. When you want to lord it over others, to be recognized, to receive adulation, you're in spiritual trouble.

The Scriptures declare,

For everyone to whom much is given, from him much will be required; and to whom much has been committed, of him they will ask the more.

Luke 12:48

The more authority you have, the more responsibility you have. Some of us want the authority, but we would rather not have the responsibility. It's fine to want a big beautiful house in a nice neighborhood, but with it come many responsibilities. For example, with the bigger house come more taxes, increased insurance costs, more grass to mow, and more space to maintain—just to mention a few.

And if you can't do all the work yourself, then you have to pay someone else to do it.

Many pray, "Lord, bless me with a Mercedes," until they find out what the personal property taxes are on such a vehicle and what it costs in maintenance. The bigger your blessing is, the bigger your responsibility to maintain that blessing will be.

Be careful when you have a desire to have some other person's position or title because there is so much behind it that you cannot know about. If you did know, you might think twice about wanting to replace that person.

Again, this temptation can take many other forms, but this gives us a good idea of what is involved.

Sensual Temptation

The third face temptation can wear is something we're all familiar with. I call it sensual temptation. It's just what it sounds like. It is lust for a person's body—to have and to enjoy what is not one's own—either legally or morally. Bonhoeffer said something very interesting about this type of temptation. He talked about how, when you're at a point that you're overtaken with sensual temptation, you're not even in a position to make a proper decision. In other words, suddenly you become willing to take everything you've worked for and put it on the line. Later, when the temptation has passed, whether you failed or passed (and most fail), you will come to your senses and say, "What on earth was I thinking?"

You'll look at yourself in the mirror one day and say, "You really need to get it together. Was it worth it—taking everything and putting it on the line for a few fleeting moments of passion?"

LIVING THE DREAM

Of these three prominent faces of temptation, this one is the more common one, affecting the lives of many Christians today. In His Word, God gave us that classic example of Joseph in Egypt.

As we saw in an earlier chapter, Joseph was blessed in his father's house, blessed in the pit, blessed in the hands of the Midianites who had bought him from his brothers, and blessed in the house of Potiphar, who subsequently bought him in the slave market. It was at this point that the enemy attacked Joseph with sensual temptation. As we discussed before, this is just the devil. Just when things are going well for us, just when we're prospering and being favored, he shows up with a temptation like this.

Joseph had the courage and the discipline to refuse. He did not want to disappoint his master, and he also didn't want to disappoint the Lord.

The woman wouldn't take no for an answer, and she kept bothering him day after day. Joseph kept refusing day after day. One day it all came to a head, and she grabbed him by his cloak and tried to force him to submit to her wishes. But Joseph was smart. He left the garments in her hands, and he ran. I like that. That's what you should do too. Run as fast as you can.

Of course, the woman was enraged and determined to do Joseph harm. She lied about him to her husband and caused him to be wrongfully imprisoned. But God vindicated him by prospering him in the prison and eventually raising him up from there to serve as the prime minister of the greatest nation on the face of the earth at the time. It was the fulfillment of a long-held dream, and Joseph had not allowed the enemy to steal it from him through yielding to temptation.

With greater success at anything in life comes greater trust, and with that greater trust comes greater vulnerability. The more successful you become, the more people will trust you, and the more people trust you, the more vulnerable you become to temptation.

Joseph was trusted by Potiphar. He had been successful even before he got to Potiphar's house, but he was successful there too, and it brought on a greater vulnerability.

The devil is not after a bum, and he doesn't attack visionless saints. He reserves his attacks for those who know that the benefits of God are upon their lives. That's why he targeted Joseph, and he will target you too.

Thomas Carlyle, a British historian and essayist, is credited with saying, "Adversity is hard on a man, but for the one who can stand prosperity, there are one hundred who can stand adversity." By this he meant that the temptations that accompany prosperity are far more and far greater than the temptations that accompany adversity. Anyone can resist when hard circumstances make it necessary, but can you resist temptation when life is easy?

You see, the more prosperous you become, the more your temptations will increase. There are many temptations that cost money, and the more money you have, the more temptations are available to you.

A poor man can't afford a sin that costs hundreds of dollars, but a rich man can spend that much and not even miss it. The only reason some of us have not experienced prosperity on the level we desire is that God knows we couldn't handle it.

As you become more prosperous and successful, your peers change. The quality of the people around you changes. Consequently, at every new level there's a new devil. And when you reach the height of success, that's where the really big demons are to be found. The temptations that accompany prosperity are far greater than the temptations that accompany adversity.

LIVING THE DREAM

Why was Joseph such a target for the devil? It was because he had been given great authority. He was handsome, and he caught women's eyes, but more than that, he was a total package. He had it all going. He was successful, and he was favored.

It is common knowledge that public figures—politicians, sports heroes, and movie stars, in particular—are subjected to much more temptation than the average person. These people have hordes of groupies around them constantly, eager and willing to give themselves to take advantage of celebrity.

With recognition come some other things—not all of them good. Joseph now had new temptations, but he refused.

Why did God take up space in the Holy Bible with this story about Potiphar's wife? He wanted to let us see that Joseph refused, so that when you and I are in similar situations, we'll know that we have power to refuse too. You can do it.

Now, concerning sensual temptation and what we have learned about what temptation is and how it works, we might ask ourselves how Joseph was able to refuse this woman. According to our text verse from James, it was because there was no desire on the inside of Joseph.

Joseph not only refused her once; he refused her many times. And you, too, can refuse to sin. You, too, can turn back temptation.

The devil, however, doesn't give up easily. Just because he did not get you on Monday doesn't mean that he'll give up. He'll come back again and again, sweetening the pot a little each time, trying to get you to bite. He knows that there are some days when you're not as strong as you are on other days.

Day after day, he came after Joseph. Day after day, day after day... Every day he used this powerful and prominent woman to tempt the young man, but still he refused. *"When desire has conceived, it gives birth to sin, and sin, when it is full-grown, brings forth*

136

death." But Joseph didn't give it a chance to conceive. He nipped it in the bud.

If there's no desire, nothing comes forth. This should lead us all to pray, "Lord, take away any wrong desire that I have."

You have no idea what the person next to you desires, but the devil knows. He not only knows, but he is determined to make that desire become reality. He is determined to bring desire to the point of yielding.

Just because you have successfully resisted a temptation does not mean that it will never reappear. It will come back, but if there is no desire, you can resist it again.

When the woman approached Joseph the first time, he refused her. At that point, common sense would have told her to move on. But it isn't like the devil to do that. Instead, Joseph became a challenge for her, and she was more determined than ever to have him. Sometimes when you resist someone, that motivates the person even more.

Many times, when we resist the devil, he just takes the battle to another level. If you're worth it to him, he'll try anything to get you. Again, he doesn't want just anybody. He wants those who are respected, those who have influence, those who are successful.

How Should We Treat Those Who Have Fallen into Temptation?

Far too many of us church folk don't yet know how to treat our brothers and sisters who have fallen into temptation. In many churches, these people are kicked simply because they happen to be down at the moment. They're judged and condemned, and few people are willing to show them any love.

"He should know better," people say. "I thought he was a preacher." "She was up there singing in the choir." "He was right there trying to pose as a righteous deacon." But God has not called us to bring condemnation upon our fellow believers. There's something the Scriptures tell us to do when we find people overtaken in a fault, and it's not criticize them and put them down even further. It's to restore them in any way we can first, and, second, to be careful lest we also be tempted ourselves:

> *Brethren, if a man is overtaken in any trespass, you who are spiritual restore such a one in a spirit of gentleness, considering yourself lest you also be tempted.*
>
> Galatians 6:1

If you've never experienced a certain temptation, it may be hard for you to feel compassion for those who do. But when you've been there, you can understand.

When someone loses a loved one, we pass by the person at the graveside, and we say, "You have my deepest sympathies." But do we really mean that? God's Word declares,

> *For we do not have a High Priest who cannot sympathize with our weaknesses, but was in all points tempted as we are, yet without sin.*
>
> Hebrews 4:15

How is it possible to have someone's deepest sympathy if he has never been where I am and never experienced what I'm feeling at the moment? It's impossible to really sympathize with someone unless you have sat where he now sits. If you haven't lost a loved one on a level with the loved one I just lost, how could you truly sympathize with me?

Within the body of Christ, we have no sympathy for sinners who should know better. We may love them, but only from a distance.

Learning to Deal with Temptation

The Lord has spoken to me that we must somehow close this gap between the church and the sinners, and it will not be done by standing back and telling sinners what they should not be doing. All of us have been overtaken by temptation of some kind, so we must be more understanding and helpful to those who are overtaken by temptation.

It's so easy for us to say, "That brother just needs to get off of drugs." It sounds good, but it's not that easy. It's a spiritual battle, and he's bound. His body and his mind are chemically dependent upon that drug.

Taking drugs is not something that people just enjoy doing. They don't get a thrill out of frequenting crack houses. Something on the inside of them pulls them there. It's a bondage, and if we're to help drug addicts, we must begin to sympathize with them, understanding their need for deliverance.

"How could he do that?" we wonder. "He doesn't care anything about his family." Oh, yes, he cares.

"Then how can he go out and spend his whole paycheck on drugs?" That's not what he wants to do. It's a bondage that needs to be broken. It's a spiritual battle that we need to help him win.

Just because a person is in bondage to drugs doesn't mean that he doesn't love God. He may very well love God, but his weakness is drugs. Your weakness may be something very different, but you have no right to criticize him or consign him to the pit.

"But he just needs to get really saved."

Oh, but he may already be "really saved."

How can that be when he does drugs? Well, how can other Christians love God and still rob Him by not paying their tithes? How can Christians love God and hurt His little ones by gossiping?

And on and on. What's the difference? He's in bondage to drugs, and another is in bondage to money.

"He doesn't need to be in the choir if he's struggling with something."

Well, if we judged everyone by those criteria, the choir would suddenly be emptied, and we would have no one qualified to preach or teach.

Let me say something important about teaching. I don't want anyone trying to teach me something if him himself hasn't been where I've been. If the person has never experienced it, how can he or she teach it? How can that person sympathize with my plight?

I'm able to testify that God can deliver because He delivered me. That's powerful and irrefutable testimony. I've been there, and I know what people are experiencing.

Even pastors are tempted, and I'm very glad that God knows how to sit me down and talk to me. He's my Father, and I'm His child, and He doesn't let me get away with anything. He not only convicts me every time I do something wrong, He even convicts me when I just *think* wrong.

There was a time when I could do my own thing, and it didn't bother me. But now that I belong to Him, that has all changed. Thank God for it.

When you begin to learn to deal with temptation, you will be on your way toward *Living the Dream*.

Chapter Ten

LEARNING TO PRAY

Now it came to pass, as He was praying in a certain place, when He ceased, that one of His disciples said to Him, "Lord, teach us to pray, as John also taught his disciples."

Luke 11:1

So many fine books have been written on prayer that I don't want to take much space here for the subject. But I cannot speak of destiny and purpose and of finding our place in God without discussing something about how we communicate with Him. Or, maybe I should say, how we don't communicate nearly enough with Him.

One of the greatest reasons the enemy has been able to deceive the people of God is our lack of prayer. In our church services, we have a couple of prayers, we sing about prayer, talk about prayer, and read about prayer, but most Christians actually spend very little time in prayer. And the devil knows this.

Communication is vital to any relationship. Statistics tell us that fifty-three percent of all marriage in this country end in divorce, and the most cited reason is a lack of communication. When communication is lacking, is it any wonder that a relationship fails?

I've known people who eventually divorced, not because they didn't love each other, but because they were unable to communicate their feelings. There was an invisible barrier between them that somehow seemingly could not be penetrated.

A successful marriage is based upon three solid foundations: sex, communication, and finances. If the enemy can attack you in any of these three strategic areas, your marriage is in danger. Couples, get it right. Have plenty of intimate moments, keep the lines of communication open between you, and keep your finances in order. It doesn't matter if you're saved and filled with the Holy Ghost, if you don't have these three elements working in your marriage, it may go under.

The devil understands the importance of communication, and he knows that decreased communication will adversely affect our relationship with God.

I once read something that really blessed me regarding this topic. If my memory serves me correctly, it called whatever distracts us from Bible study and prayer a "thief." These distractions steal from us. Not only do they steal blessings from us, but they also rob God of glory. Those distractions could be your job, your personal schedule, your spouse, or your child.

Because of this, the devil's objective is to keep your agenda so full that you have time for everything else but prayer. That's why every time you get on your knees before the Lord, you suddenly feel sleepy, the phone rings, and people you haven't thought about in years suddenly come to your mind. The devil will use anything at all to prevent you from praying. He hates prayer because it produces intimacy.

You cannot pray to God without giving Him glory, and when you can't pray, you rob Him of the glory He deserves.

The devil doesn't mind you going to church—just as long as you don't get serious about prayer. He doesn't mind you shouting and dancing a little—as long as you don't get serious about prayer. He doesn't even mind you reading your Bible a little—as long as you don't get serious about prayer.

And we accommodate Satan by making time for everything else but prayer. We have time to get the oil changed on our cars. We have time to clean out closets. We have time to receive visitors. We seem to have time for everything—except for God. If the devil can continue to keep the lines of communication between our Father and us cut, then he will deceive us and rob us of our destinies.

There are three important things that can change your life of prayer. Learn them and put them into practice.

The First Step Toward Successful Prayer Is to Discipline the Flesh

The first thing we need, as it relates to prayer, is to discipline ourselves. The word *discipline* comes from the same root word as *disciple*, which means "one who follows, or learns from." Being a true disciple of the Lord requires discipline.

Discipline is important to spiritual growth. Natural growth takes place automatically, but spiritual growth takes effort. To grow naturally, all you have to do is eat and stay healthy, and it will happen automatically. I have a young boy named Trey, but I don't have to stand over Trey and command him to grow. All I have to do is feed him and keep him healthy, and he grows automatically.

That's not the case with spiritual growth. If you want to grow spiritually, you have to put forth an effort. For one thing, you sometimes have to break away from old friends and have more time to yourself. This is the reason that many remain spiritual babes. They lack discipline.

The writer of Hebrews stated,

For though by this time you ought to be teachers, you need someone to teach you again the first principles of the oracles of God; and you have come to need milk and not solid food. For everyone who partakes only of milk is unskilled in the word of righteousness, for he is a babe. But solid food belongs to those who are of full age, that is, those who by reason of use have their senses exercised to discern both good and evil.

Hebrews 5:12–14

Something is wrong when a person has been saved and walking with the Lord for six to ten years already, and yet is still on milk. By now, the person ought to be eating solid foods.

When you're still a baby, any little thing hurts you and hinders you. It's time to grow up. You must establish some discipline in your life.

This means that we have to make our flesh do what it doesn't want to do. "Yes," we must insist, "I am going to pray." Unless we are firm with ourselves, it won't work. Your flesh does not want to submit to the will of God.

Set a specific time to dedicate to prayer. You might want to start with ten minutes, and later you can increase it. Once you have set the time, make your flesh obey. Even the disciples of Jesus had to learn to pray.

Learning to Pray

There are several important things that we can learn from this text. First, we find Jesus praying, despite the fact that He was the Son of God, God in the flesh, the perfect Creator. He was all of this and more, yet He took time to commune with the Father. If Jesus, the Son of God, took time to pray, what makes you think that you and I can live without doing it?

When Jesus had finished His prayers, one of His disciples came to Him and said, *"Lord, teach us to pray."* Notice that he did not say, "Teach us *how* to pray." Prayer is just talking to God, and every single one of us knows how to talk. The disciples needed Jesus to teach them *to* pray. The deficiency was not in knowing *how* to pray, but in knowing *to* pray. And that's what we need today as well. We know *how* to pray, but we're lacking the discipline to actually do it.

John the Baptist had taught his disciples to pray as well. So, this is something that we have to teach. We must discipline our flesh to do it.

Say to your flesh, "I will pray. I will pray in the morning. I will pray at noonday. I will pray at night." Start by praying sometime, anytime that is convenient. Make time for it.

Then say, "Flesh, this is our time to pray. Mind, soul, everything about me, come under subjection, stop what you're doing, and give God attention." It may sound crazy, but it works. This is the first important step toward a meaningful prayer life.

The Second Step Toward Successful Prayer Is to Move from Discipline to Desire

After discipline comes desire. At first, you force yourself, but then, when you have done that, prayer suddenly becomes your desire. Now, you can't wait for everyone to leave so that you can talk to God. You can't wait to get into your car by yourself so that you can pray. You can't wait for your break time to come so that you can commune with Him. And the more you talk to God, the greater your desire for prayer becomes.

When we move from discipline to desire, everything changes. When you say, "Father, it's me again. I know You just heard from me a few minutes ago, but I'm talking to You again. I couldn't wait," you've suddenly fallen in love with prayer, and you can't wait for your next opportunity. It is then that you start praying while you're waiting for the bus. You start praying while you're taking a shower.

When you first had to force your flesh to pray, prayer was a burden, an imposition, a task. Now, you look forward to doing it, and you want to take it to an even higher level.

The Third Step Toward Successful Prayer Is to Move from Desire to Delight

And there is a higher level. It's in moving from desire to delight. Now, you're in love with prayer because you're in love with God. Prayer has not only ceased to be a chore, but now you love to do it. It's one of your favorite things. Unlike some, you don't just do it when food is placed before you; you do it all the time, anytime.

Some people only pray when they're in trouble, but that's not successful prayer. Prayer must become our delight, so that the more we do it the more we want to do it, and, when this is true, it becomes easier and more enjoyable with each opportunity.

I'm not a super saint by any stretch of the imagination, and I still have a long way to go toward perfection, but I can tell you that when I wake up in the morning, before I greet anyone else, I turn to the Lord and thank Him. This has become my habit.

For instance, I might say, "Lord, I thank You that I slept so well last night that I didn't even know who I was. And it wasn't my alarm clock that woke me up this morning. It was You. You touched me with the finger of Your love. And, if You hadn't done that, I wouldn't have awakened."

I enjoy talking to God in the morning like that. No, I delight in talking to Him like that.

I love to pray because I know that what I ask will come to pass, and I want to watch it happen. That brings me a lot of joy. It thrills me when someone says to me, "Bishop, do you remember when I asked you for prayer, and you prayed for me? Well, I got the answer." I love it. I love it when people get healed or get a job or have some other victory as a result of my prayers. That's my joy.

Concerning prayer, our God has said,

Call to Me, and I will answer you, and show you great and mighty things, which you do not know.

Jeremiah 33:3

Ask, and it will be given to you; seek, and you will find; knock, and it will be opened to you. For everyone who asks receives, and he who seeks finds, and to him who knocks it will be opened.

Matthew 7:7–8

The Secret Password to Prayer

There are many other wonderful secrets to prayer to be found in God's Word. One of the most important of them is to be found in the words of the psalmist:

LIVING THE DREAM

Enter into His gates with thanksgiving, and into His courts with praise. Be thankful to Him, and bless His name. For the Lord is good; His mercy is everlasting, and His truth endures to all generations.

Psalm 100:4–5

Every time you pray, before you ask God for anything, you ought to just begin to thank Him. The words *thank you* are like a password that gets you into the presence of God.

Thank Him for what He's brought you through. Thank Him for what He's doing in your life right now. Even thank Him for your problems. They're helping you to be an overcomer. Thank Him for your enemies. Thank Him for your pains.

And when you have thanked Him enough, He will say to you, "Now, you can come on into My presence and tell Me what you need."

Some people want to rush into God's presence with a laundry list of petitions: "Lord, give me this. Give me that. Give me the other." But God says, "You haven't even gotten into My presence adequately. Why are you asking for all of these things?" Enter by praising Him. Then, at His invitation, you can make your petitions known.

Sometimes, before you know it, a whole hour will have gone by, and you will still be thanking God for the things He has done for you today. Then there's yesterday and the day before and last week and last month and last year.

Eventually you'll look back over your whole life and thank Him for everything you've gone through—even when you didn't understand it at the time. We should never run out of things to praise God for.

Learning to Pray

When you come to God in this way, you need not be concerned about using religious phrases. Just talk to Him out of your heart. Before you know it, your heavy burdens will have lifted, and you will know that you are in His presence.

It would be wise for each of us to ask the Lord teach us to pray. In my own life, nothing has been more important to my success, and, for that reason, Satan has fought it with all his strength.

After I have told God about my problems, in the natural, they may still look the same. But I know on the inside that something has happened. The songwriter wrote, "Oh, what needless pain we bear, all because we do not carry everything to God in prayer."

We come to God with something on our hearts, something on our minds. We've been worrying about it, we've been telling our companions at work about it, and we've been talking to our children about it. We've told everyone else about it except God. As the songwriter said, we're bearing "needless" pain. We often carry such pains all day long and all week long—"all because we do not [or will not] carry everything to God in prayer."

Friend, learn to pray, and you'll be on the road to *Living the Dream*.

LIVING THE DREAM

Chapter Eleven

LEARNING TO HANDLE STRESS

Not that I speak in regard to need, for I have learned in what-
ever state I am, to be content: I know how to be abased, and I
know how to abound. Everywhere and in all things I have
learned [am instructed, KJV] both to be full and to be hungry,
both to abound and to suffer need. I can do all things through
Christ who strengthens me.

Philippians 4:11–13

I personally feel that the Gospel has an answer for every problem, and that in it we should be able to find an answer to anything
and everything we experience in life. I see here in the words of
Paul to the Philippian church an answer for how you and I, as
believers in the Lord Jesus Christ, can remove stress from our
lives. All of us periodically have to deal with stress. Even if you are

saved and sanctified and filled with the Holy Ghost, you still have to learn to handle stress.

This problem of stress has become a huge issue of our day. Medical doctors have proven that stress can bring on physical ailments. It can literally affect every area of your anatomy. And God has an answer for it.

What is stress? Stress is mental, emotional, or physical tension; it is mental, emotional, or physical strain. It is brought on by many factors. It can be job related, or it can be caused by family problems, financial problems, or even school problems. Generally speaking, it is caused by having to deal with the circumstances of life.

The amazing thing is to know the circumstances in which Paul was writing this letter. He was imprisoned in Rome, and, as he wrote, he was sitting chained in a dungeon waiting for the neurotic emperor Nero to wake up one day and decide that it was the time to remove his head. His life was literally in the hands of this mentally unbalanced man.

It was dark and cold in that dungeon, and Paul was uncomfortable and couldn't have been feeling his best. All in all, it would be hard to imagine a more stressful situation than that. And yet, in the midst of those circumstances, the apostle wrote, "I am content."

Some have played down the role of contentment in the Christian life, but they're wrong to do that. God intended for us to be content. It's the greatest feeling in the world. To be content is to have a mind free from anxiety, free from depression, and free from all thought of troubles.

But Paul was not free of trouble, was he? The trouble was there; it was just not accompanied by the normal stress. So why was that? There's a truth to be found here, and if we can lay hold of it, our lives can move to a whole new level. The ability to live a life of contentment free from the stress of everyday life is one to be sought.

Learning to Flow with the Season

To my way of thinking, to be content simply means to flow with the season. The great preacher of Ecclesiastes wrote,

To everything there is a season, a time for every purpose under heaven.

Ecclesiastes 3:1

Seasons come and seasons go, and I've come to accept that whatever I'm experiencing right now has come about because this is the season for me to go through it. So, instead of being dragged down by the circumstances, I choose to just flow with them. Life has a way of placing us in many uncomfortable situations, but as we learn to deal with them as a passing season, we are victorious.

Somehow I feel that this was how Paul looked upon this period of his life. Most assuredly, he had bruises on his back. After all, he was being persecuted on every hand. But still, he was content.

This was especially not easy because he was such an important man. He had begun as a tentmaker in his early Christian service, but he had gone on to become a globetrotting messenger for the church. Eventually, he would write some two-thirds of the New Testament scriptures. Now he has been placed in the most difficult of circumstances, and he had the grace to say that he didn't want anyone to feel sorry for him.

Paul knew that his days were numbered, that he had about finished his course on earth. But, before he got out of that prison, he hoped that what he was enduring would help others who found themselves in the same situation. So, he wrote the words of this letter.

Paul wasn't trying to get something from his readers; he was trying to share something that he had learned. He had learned that he could be content in whatever state he found himself. He had learned to flow with the season.

He went on to say that he had lived a balanced life. He now knew how to be abased and how to abound, how to be full and how to be hungry, how to have plenty and how to suffer need. He knew what it felt like to be exalted, or uplifted, and he also knew what it felt like to be put down and be humiliated. Now, after experiencing all of that, he was writing to say that he was still content.

Once you get this revelation into your spirit and begin to apply it to the events of your daily life, you will be able to handle all the stresses that come your way. Stress will no longer have dominion over you.

In order to be content when you're down, you first have to know how to be content when you're up. That's the problem with many of those who, as we say, "have arrived." Once they arrive, they forget where they came from. That's dangerous. You might be on your high horse today, but don't get too comfortable because the same God who took you up can bring you back down.

Paul had learned something. He knew how to act when every-thing was going well. He could handle it. When people had their arms around him, he didn't let it excite him too much. He knew that not everyone who patted him on the back was pleased with his progress. So he knew to stay humble when he was on top.

If any man had a reason to boast, it was Paul. But he wasn't about to do it. When they tried to tell him how great he was, he responded,

Learning to Handle Stress

It is no longer I who live, but Christ lives in me; and the life which I now live in the flesh I live by faith in the Son of God, who loved me and gave Himself for me.

Galatians 2:20

When you give God the praise, when you give Him the glory for everything in your life and get it out of your head that it's you, then your life will go to another level. That's why God can't bless some people. As soon as He blesses them and lifts them up and men begin to pat them on the back, they begin to rob God of the glory due Him. They act like they deserve what they got, but if the truth were to be told, everything that we have came from God. We are where we are only because He brought us this far. And we can advance further only as He takes us onward.

Give God the glory, and never take it for yourself. He performs His miracles for those who recognize that only He could have done it. Because He can't use proud people, there are many that He simply can't bless. As soon as they get two pork chops above poverty, as we say, their nose goes in the air.

Being Instructed

When Paul said, *"I have learned both to be full and to be hungry, both to abound and to suffer need,"* the phrase *"I have learned"* in the King James Version of the Bible is translated *"I am instructed."* His response was not automatic. He refused to take the glory for himself because he had been taught not to do it.

Thank God for the Holy Ghost who teaches us! He is saying to us today that we will have some full days, and we will have some empty days. Sometimes we will be rich, and at other times we may be poor. Sometimes we will be hungry, and at other times we will be full.

155

LIVING THE DREAM

Hunger is not a bad thing sometimes. Physical hunger causes us to go on a spiritual eating spree. When there's no food on the table, no money in the bank, and our backs are up against a wall, we find ourselves praying more than we've ever prayed before. So it's a good thing.

When we get a little too high, a little too proud, God knows how to bring us down. He lets a little trouble come into our lives because when we don't have any troubles, we don't praise Him nearly enough. When we don't have any troubles, we're too busy for prayer. So every now and then God has to say, "I know what you need. A little trouble is coming your way."

When there's trouble in your life, you'll find yourself on your face more before God. People who have never been though any tests and trials have no reason to pray. But when the bottom falls out, and you look around for those who were supposed to be standing by you side and they're gone, you quickly learn how to talk to God.

Oh, yes, those people will be standing around you as long as things are going well, but when things go wrong, they disappear like Houdini. When you need them the most, they're nowhere to be found. And that's just what you need, so that you can learn to trust God more.

You tried to be there for them when they needed you, but for some strange reason they can't return the favor. But just thank the Lord that He's teaching you to trust Him. He periodically leaves the windows of adversity open over your life to teach you stay on your knees. The Lord knows how to get your attention.

The Test

There will be a test. Every time you are taught something, afterward the test is sure to come. So, don't just shout off the teaching. Get ready to pass the test.

156

Learning to Handle Stress

If you hear someone quote the truth, "No weapon that's formed against me will prosper," you may be able to know where it's found in the Scriptures, but you still have to pass the test. When God allows a weapon to be raised over you, it's not to threaten your life. It's to see if you can pass the test.

You may think that God has forgotten about you. It may look like He's blessing everybody else but you, but it's only a test. You're crying, but it's only a test. It's not to destroy you. It's only a test.

After you've been tested, just as in school, you can then go on to the next level. The devil is so dumb. If he had good sense, he would leave us alone. His tests just prepare us for the next level.

Satan doesn't understand that the more we have to go through, the more we're going to call on God. And the more God delivers us, the more faith we're going to have in Him. When you come out of your current test, you'll be shouting as never before. If you are dancing now, you'll really be dancing then.

If you have truly learned, then you should be able to reach in and pull out what you have learned in the moment it is needed. Then you can say to the devil, "This is only a test. I don't have time to be laid low by stress. I have too much to do. God has been too good to me for me to be walking the floors all night long. Why should I be worrying myself to death over something I can't even control?"

And what are we worried about, anyway? Just go with the flow. There's no reason to be stressed, with your blood pressure elevated and your nerves taut and you not sleeping at night. It's only a test.

The Stress-Free Life Is Based on the Goodness and Faithfulness of God

Behold, He who keeps Israel shall neither slumber nor sleep.
Psalm 121:4

If God is going to be up anyway, why don't you go on to sleep? It doesn't make sense for both of you to stay up. He is so good and faithful that you can trust Him and go on to sleep without a worry in the world.

Paul believed in the goodness of the Lord, and that allowed him to remain content—regardless of what he had to go through. He could flow with the season because he knew God.

If you know anything about seasons, you know that they come and they go. So this season of your life won't last forever. Things will change. And if you know anything at all about God, you know that He never changes. So rest easy in His love.

The number one killer today is not AIDS. It's not cancer. It's not some plague. The number one killer is ignorance about the goodness of God. His Word declares,

My people are destroyed for lack of knowledge.

Hosea 4:6

That's why the devil doesn't want people to attend good churches where they can learn about God. He knows that if they listen and learn, they will be able to pass the test when the time comes.

Some of us have learned to keep praising God—even when we don't have a dime in our pockets and we don't know where our next meal is coming from. We can still praise Him because we have learned, and we can pass the test.

Paul was "instructed." Jesus said,

Take My yoke upon you and learn from Me, for I am gentle and lowly in heart, and you will find rest for your souls.

Matthew 11:29

158

Learning to Handle Stress

"Learn from Me." Jesus had a stress-free life. Paul learned to have a stress-free life. And you, too, can have a stress-free life.

The Teacher

After you've established a relationship with God through the person of the Holy Spirit, you may, as we say, "get down," but you won't stay down long. According to the Word of God, the Holy Ghost becomes your Teacher:

> *These things I have spoken to you while being present with you. But the Helper, the Holy Spirit, whom the Father will send in My name, He will teach you all things, and bring to your remembrance all things that I said to you.*
>
> John 14:25–26

"If you establish a relationship with Me," Jesus was saying, "you are then My child, and I will prepare you for every test. My Spirit will teach you and will bring to your memory all the things I have taught you."

That's why, when I get down and burdened, I can't stay that way for long. The Holy Ghost brings something to my remembrance that will carry me through any dark night. When men lie about me, the Holy Ghost brings something to my remembrance that sets me free from the sadness of it. When people scandalize my name, the Holy Ghost brings something back to me that allows me to bear it and remain calm and content.

This will work for any of us. If a doctor tell you that there's nothing more that he can do to help you, the Holy Ghost will remind you of God's promise to heal. When you're feeling lonely, He can give you something that will comfort you. Jesus said of the Spirit,

LIVING THE DREAM

And I will pray the Father, and He will give you another Helper,
that He may abide with you forever—the Spirit of truth, whom
the world cannot receive, because it neither sees Him nor knows
Him; but you know Him, for He dwells with you and will be in
you. I will not leave you orphans; I will come to you.

John 14:16–18

The Comforter teaches us that we can't get too excited when things are going well for us. We love the sunshine, but there are some dark days coming too. The sun doesn't shine every day. Some days are cloudy, and others are stormy.

We must learn to be content in any state, under any condition, in any situation. And we can do it by reaching inside us and pulling out something that we have learned, some of the reserve that is stored up within us. With God's promises, we can face any and every problem that comes our way.

When the moment arrives to go through the test, the Holy Ghost will be faithful, and He will bring forth something out of your spirit. Someone may have asked Paul, for instance, "What happens when you're feeling lonely?"

I can hear Paul saying in response, "That's when the Holy Ghost will reach back and remind me of the promise of Psalm 27:10..."

When my father and my mother forsake me, then the LORD will
take care of me.

Psalm 27:10

"Paul, what happens when you're facing death?"

"That's when the Spirit reaches back and brings to me the words of Psalm 23:4..."

Learning to Handle Stress

Yea, though I walk through the valley of the shadow of death, I will fear no evil; for You are with me; Your rod and Your staff, they comfort me.

Psalm 23:4

"Paul, what happens if Nero decides to cut your head off?"

"Then I'll reach in with the Spirit and draw out 1 Thessalonians 4:13–14..."

But I do not want you to be ignorant, brethren, concerning those who have fallen asleep, lest you sorrow as others who have no hope. For if we believe that Jesus died and rose again, even so God will bring with Him those who sleep in Jesus.

1 Thessalonians 4:13–14

"Paul, how do find the courage to react with calm when men are against you?"

"Then I'll reach in by the Spirit and get out Romans 8:31..."

What then shall we say to these things? If God is for us, who can be against us?

Romans 8:31

"Paul, what happens when you cannot hold back your tears?"

"Then I'll reach in by the Spirit and get what Revelation 21:4 says..."

And God will wipe away every tear from their eyes; there shall be no more death, nor sorrow, nor crying. There shall be no more pain, for the former things have passed away.

Revelation 21:4

LIVING THE DREAM

Paul had enough stored up in him to enable him to pass every test, and you do too. Friend, it's not enough just to shout; it's not enough just to dance. You need the Word of God down deep inside you and you need the Comforter to bring it to your remembrance. It's what will sustain you.

As you learn to live a stress-free life, you are taking another giant step toward *Living the Dream.*

Chapter Twelve

LEARNING TO FIND FREEDOM FROM FAKE FRIENDS

Therefore I will look to the LORD; I will wait for the God of my salvation; my God will hear me. Do not rejoice over me, my enemy; when I fall, I will arise; when I sit in darkness, the LORD will be a light to me. I will bear the indignation of the LORD, because I have sinned against Him, until He pleads my case and executes justice for me. He will bring me forth to the light; I will see His righteousness. Then she who is my enemy will see, and shame will cover her who said to me, "Where is the LORD your God?" My eyes will see her; now she will be trampled down like mire in the streets.

Micah 7:7–10

Micah, because it is the thirty-third book of the Bible and is not very big, is one of the most overlooked of the great books of

the Bible. It is pregnant with untapped truths. The book express-
es the purpose of God in bringing His chosen people back into
conformity with His will and plan. Israel had strayed and gotten
off course, and God used Micah to sound a warning to bring them
back to their rightful position in Him.

One of the great privileges I enjoy through reading my Bible is
to get up close and personal with some of the people who truly
walked with God. Nothing can do that like the Bible. We can't go
by what we see in churches because what we're seeing there are
dressed-up personalities. They're not only dressed up physically,
but they're also dressed up mentally and emotionally. The real
person is often hidden under all that disguise. When we look at
the Word of God, we see the naked truth. We see people just as
they were.

This glimpse into the intimate life of other saints has been an
important point of comparison for me to my own existence. I can
better understand my own life because of seeing how others
lived.

It has been very important to me to know that these are not wax
figures, some strange and unique characters. They're real men and
women just like me, and they experienced all the passions of life. I
can learn from their experience only because they went through
some of the same things I go through on a daily basis.

Satan Is a Master of Perversion

In this chapter, I want to expose the enemy as a master at perverting what God's originates. Satan is an expert at taking a picture, one of God's originals, and running off a copy of it that is
changed so slightly as to make it look authentic. It is clearly an
impostor, but if you don't know the real thing well, you would
never detect the deception.

Learning to Find Freedom from Fake Friends

This is the devil's job, and he's good at it. He loves to pervert the plan of God, and his perversions can be seen throughout the Bible. Everything God does, the devil comes along and tries to repeat it in some perverted way.

This is why I love the story of Calvary so much. It was there that Jesus beat the devil at his own game. The devil had used a woman, a man, and a tree to place us into bondage, and Jesus used a woman, a man, and a tree to set us free. I can hear the Lord saying to Satan afterward, "I just beat you at your own game."

The devil found a woman named Eve, a man named Adam, and a tree known as the tree of the knowledge of good and evil, and he used them all to place us into bondage. The Lord found a woman named Mary, a man named Jesus, and a tree set on Calvary's hill, and He used them all to set us free. Thank God!

The devil is a perverted character. God tells us to go after love, but the devil tells us to go after lust. And lust is nothing more than perverted love. To pervert something means to twist it until it becomes a spin-off of the original. It may look much like the original, but it's fake. There is such a thing as fake friendship, and that's the very subject I want to deal with.

God often sends a person into your life who can make it turn for the better, but the devil often sends a person into your life who can make it turn for the worse. The devil takes the things God has instituted for good and, perverting them, uses them to destroy. This is what he does with fake friendships.

We all are products of our relationships—whether they be relationships between mother and daughter, father and son, husband and wife, girlfriend and boyfriend, or just friends or colleagues. To this end, God strategically places people into our lives who can bless us. He gives us true friends. Satan does just the opposite. He places false friends into our lives, hoping that they will influence us for evil.

These people may seem to have all the attributes of a friend, and they may do many good things for us. But underneath it all, they're really enemies in disguise, and the long-term result of their friendship is our spiritual loss.

Far too many of us cling to professed friends, whether God has sent them or not. We so desperately want to be accepted, loved, and appreciated that we grasp at any offered friendship, and the results are often tragic.

We love to fit into our little circles of friends, so whenever a new offer of friendship comes along, we jump at the chance. But not every friend is really a friend.

Most of us never like to be alone. We so long for companionship that we find activities that we can do with other people around us. For example, we always want someone to go to a restaurant with us. Because of this, we become too gullible and accept anyone who poses as a friend.

The worst thing about this is that when we think we have discovered a new friend, we often, as we say, "spill our guts" to these people, telling them everything about us, revealing the secrets of our hearts and exposing all our pains. Having known these people only a short time, we open up our whole lives to them and stand before them as naked as we could possibly be. This might feel good at the moment, but it's not wise.

People who have only spoken together on the phone are suddenly eating out together and feeling that God has placed them into each other's lives. And they couldn't possibly really know each other yet. Then, a few months down the road, they suddenly discover that the person they were so happy to meet has not made their lives better, but actually worse. Only then, when it's too late, do they realize that that "friend" was sent by the devil himself. That person were not placed into their lives to elevate them, but to drag them back.

Are we so gullible as to think that everyone with a smile on his face is really happy with us and loving us? I hope not, because it's not that way at all.

Let's take this a step further. Even those whom we meet in church, who smile in our faces and give us their warm hands, or even hug us firmly or kiss us, may be stabbing us in the back at the same time. Are there backstabbers in churches? Oh, yes, there are. And God wants to set us free from such fake friends.

If you haven't learned it already, you should know that you must be careful whom you get close to. Be careful about whom you call your friend. Be even more careful about whom you call your "best" friend. That best friend has a best friend, and that best friend has a best friend, and on and on it goes. And if your best friend talks to her best friend, and that best friend talks to another best friend, soon you will find that your innermost secrets have become common knowledge.

If a best friend is talking about one of their other friends around you, what do you think he or she will do when around others? That friend tell all of your secrets too.

God knows how to place people in your life to bless you, but the devil knows how to place people in your life to curse you. This thought may disturb those who have been single for years and who now feel that they have finally found the right person for marriage. This is serious. You don't want to make a mistake. You don't make things even worse. You don't want to bring even more grief upon your life. So be very careful.

Think long and hard about the people you are spending your time with. Are they true friends? Or are they perhaps Satan's emissaries in disguise?

I've had people smile in my face and then go out and lie about me like a dog, and we don't need friends like that. I might expect that kind of treatment from an infidel, but we expect better of those we call "Brother" or "Sister."

The apostle Paul experienced this. When he needed the support of his friends, they were nowhere to be found. I'm sure that you've been hurt in this way as well. All of us have.

When people you trusted and people you confided in turn against you, that hurts. Micah lamented,

The faithful man has perished from the earth, and there is no one upright among men.

Micah 7:2

Good people are had to find these days. Micah went on:

That they may successfully do evil with both hands...

Micah 7:3

In other words, the people in verse 3 were alive to make others miserable. Whether you know it yet or not, there is somebody who is anointed to get on your nerves. That person is anointed to pull you down, anointed to sap your spiritual strength. If you're not careful, you'll find yourself wasting your time with someone who really means you no good. That's why the Bible declares,

But earnestly desire the best gifts. And yet I show you a more excellent way.

1 Corinthians 12:31

What are *"the best gifts"*? Discernment is certainly one that we all could use more of. We should be so discerning in the spirit that when we come into the company of a certain person, and that person is not of the spirit, the Holy Ghost will expose it to us immediately and forcefully.

The person may be smiling and looking good and saying the same things everyone else is saying, but when he or she gets close to you, you feel something wrong, and you instinctively know to avoid that person. If we allow the Spirit of God to do it, He will make us sensitive to phoniness. He's certainly not fooled by fakes, and He can help us not to be fooled by them either.

The Spirit of God and the spirit of evil don't mix. And God is never taken by surprise by anyone's attitude. He knows a phony when He sees one.

Sometimes the people we do the most for are the ones who betray us, and there can be no doubt that the most difficult hurts to overcome are those caused by the people closest to us. I know people who have never gotten over a divorce, for example. They put so much trust in that man or that woman, that when the betrayal came, they were devastated and never recovered.

People who are that close to us certainly know more about us than anyone else because we have shared with them our most intimate secrets. But there's more to it than that. We trusted them as a friend, and they let us down. Micah said,

> *Do not trust in a friend; do not put your confidence in a companion.*
>
> Micah 7:5

Real Friends

Then, how do we know who our real friends are? We need to know because if the people close to us are not all real friends, this places us in serious danger.

A person who is a real friend is someone who sincerely doesn't mind you having what he or she has. This could be something material or something spiritual. If you call yourself my friend and you can't rejoice when I get blessed, then you were never really my friend to begin with.

If I'm your friend, I want to see you blessed. If I'm your friend, then I want to see you have everything that God has promised you. If I'm your friend, I would never be jealous of you or of what you have. If your "friend" doesn't like you anymore because you've been blessed, then that person was never a real friend.

Jesus said,

Greater love has no one than this, than to lay down one's life for his friends.

John 15:13

If I'm your friend, I would be willing to give my very life for you, for I sincerely want you to have what I have.

That's how I know that Jesus is my Friend. He wants me to have all the best. He's anointed, and so He wants me to be anointed too. Since He's my friend, He's not happy when the devil is destroying me and I'm walking around powerless. Jesus isn't defeated and powerless, and He wants me to have everything that He has.

The wonderful thing is that if I want it, He wants me to have it. I want His power to cast out demons. I want His power to tread on serpents and scorpions. I want His power to look the devil square in the eyes and defy him. I want His anointing so that whomever I lay hands on will recover. And we can all have it—if we're His friends. He wants us to have it.

We know that He's our Savior, but do we know that He's our Friend?

170

Learning to Find Freedom from Fake Friends

Those of us who have close friends understand that it's a very special relationship. There are associates, and there are friends, and there's a difference. A friend can have the shirt off of your back.

A friend is not necessarily someone with whom you talk on the telephone every night. You may not talk for months at a time, but when your back is against the wall, you know that a friend is only a phone call away.

Good friends are hard to find. If you have one, you'd better cherish him or her. There's no surplus of friendship in the world today—not real friendship anyway.

Many people know how to be polite, to smile and greet you, or to pat you on the back. But watch them change when God begins to bless you. You're wasting your time with some of them right now, and they're a hindrance to your progress. You may not recognize it now, but when God blesses you, you'll see that they don't rejoice with you. Instead, they'll be jealous because they don't want you to have something they don't have.

"Do not trust in a friend," Micah wrote. Don't trust in anyone whom you only think is a friend, and always test friendship before you entrust too much.

When Friendships End

Not every friendship that ends does so because it wasn't a true friendship. God sometimes allows ruptured relationships to reveal the risen Redeemer. He has to let relationships that we have invested a lot in to go bad sometimes so that we can really come to know who He is.

But, more often than not, when friendships go bad, it's because they were never true friendships to start with. Oh, if that "no good man" could only see you now! He was sure that when it was all

171

over, you wouldn't be worth anything. But God had to separate you from him so that you could come to know that He was the only real Man and that nobody could treat you as well as He could. So dry your eyes and stop crying about what you lost. What you perceive as loss is really gain.

I'm so glad when God exposes some of the people I've been wasting my time with. The next time I see them, I find that I have little time to spend. They've wasted enough of my time already. I need to move on to greater things.

Many of the people who now call themselves your friends will not be accompanying you to your final destination. Let me explain what I mean.

Once I was on my way to preach in Baltimore. My ticket showed two places, the city where I would board (New Orleans) and my destination (Baltimore). In parenthesis, it said, "One stop," but I didn't pay any attention to that.

On the flight out of New Orleans, I fell asleep and woke up only when the plane was landing. I reached into the overhead compartment, took out my bags, and started to get off of the plane. Just then one of the flight attendants, who just happened to be a member of our church, said, "Bishop, are you getting off here?"

"Yes," I said. "I have to preach in Baltimore."

"Wait a minute, Bishop," she answered. "This is not Baltimore; this is Cincinnati."

"What?" I asked, startled. "Am I on the wrong flight? I need to go to Baltimore."

"No," she assured me, "you're on the right flight. This is just a stopover."

Learning to Find Freedom from Fake Friends

In that moment, the Spirit of God began to speak to me and show me that I was not yet at my final spiritual destination either. My current spiritual location was just a stopover.

Why did it happen? Well, in the case of the plane, maybe it needed a refueling stop. I'm not sure. Was it just picking up additional passengers? Maybe. But there was a purpose. I didn't know what it was, but I had to trust that the airline officials knew. So I took a few minutes and went into the Cincinnati airport before proceeding.

Eventually, I came to the conclusion that our stop in Cincinnati was to let certain people off, and that spoke to me. There are people in your life who will not be accompanying you to your final destination. They're simply not going where you're going, so God has to let them off at some point. Don't worry about it. This is just a stopover. Some are getting off here, but you're going on.

That bad divorce you went though was just a stopover en route to your final destination. Being fired from your job was just a stopover en route to your final destination. Don't confuse this stopover with your final destination. You're not there yet.

Make up your mind that you're going all the way and that no matter whom you lose along the way, you will not settle with less than God's best for your own life.

Tell the devil, "I'm not getting off yet. This is not my final destination. Some people may get off here, but I'm not. Others may miss the final destination, but I'm determined not to miss it. I know what God promised me, and on the way to receiving it, I will rejoice in His promise—whatever others do."

It's time to say good-bye to some of your fake friends. Let them move aside, and let God give you some real friends who will rejoice when the Lord picks you up.

173

LIVING THE DREAM

You may have to change your phone number. You may have to tear up your phone book. You don't have time to waste with those who can't rejoice when you get blessed.

This is your season, and you're in for some big changes. Some of those changes involve those whom you have called "friend." Let them go and move on toward your final destination.

This is just a stopover. If you keep your joy, if you keep your peace, if you keep a smile on your face, you'll make it to your next stop.

It was only at this point that Micah arrived at our text verse for this chapter and exulted: *"Therefore I will look to the LORD; I will wait for the God of my salvation."* Let this also be your determination. Don't be in such a hurry to give out your phone number to the people you meet. Don't be in a hurry to get someone riding with you in your car. Don't be in a hurry to find a companion for your lonely hours. Wait on the Lord and allow Him to send the right people your way.

Then Micah was really inspired and said, *"Do not rejoice over me, my enemy."* When you go through something, there are those who are glad. But they'd better be careful about rejoicing when you fall, for you're coming up again. It's one thing to be down and stay down, but you're going to get back up and go on.

Until now, God has allowed you to get back up. You could have been sleeping in your grave already long ago, but He gave you another chance, and another, and another. And if He is for you, then who can be against you? So, you're coming out of this current crisis too.

Praise God for some of those broken relationships. Thank Him because some of the people you called friend are no longer in your life. If they had been, you wouldn't have what you have today. Thank Him because you could have married the wrong man or woman, but God wouldn't let it happen because that was your layover, not your final destination.

You thought you were so much in love, but aren't you glad that God knew your future? He knew where He was going to take you. He knew what the final outcome would be.

If it had been left up to us, we would have made the wrong choices. We didn't know which door to pick. Was it door number one, door number two, or door number three? I certainly didn't know which one to pick, but God did.

Sometimes He shuts all three doors. Then we walk away and have to wait on God. That's good. Don't listen to people's advice. They can't give you a good husband or wife. Only God can do that. Wait on Him.

Look for some more shake-ups in your relationships, as you learn to be free from fake friends and further your progress toward *Living the Dream*.

LIVING THE DREAM

Chapter Thirteen

LEARNING TO AVOID
QUITTING

And Ahab told Jezebel all that Elijah had done, also how he had executed all the prophets with the sword. Then Jezebel sent a messenger to Elijah, saying, "So let the gods do to me, and more also, if I do not make your life as the life of one of them by tomorrow about this time." And when he saw that, he arose and ran for his life, and he went to Beersheba, which belongs to Judah and left his servant there. But he himself went a day's journey into the wilderness, and came and sat down under a broom tree. And he prayed that he might die, and said, "It is enough! Now, LORD, take my life, for I am no better than my fathers."...So he said, "I have been very zealous for the LORD God of hosts; for the children of Israel have forsaken Your covenant, torn down Your altars, and killed Your prophets with a sword. I alone am left; and they seek to take my life."

1 Kings 19:1–4, 10

LIVING THE DREAM

In a previous chapter, we looked at this passage in a different context, one which concerned the prevalence of the spirit of depression. Here we are interested in Elijah's apparent decision to quit.

Be honest now. Haven't you wanted to quit at some point? Most of us have, and many of us have felt like quitting many times. We may use the term "throwing in the towel" or "giving up." It all means the same.

This doesn't necessarily mean that we are quitting God. Often it means that we feel like giving up on some particular promise that He has made. It just seems too difficult for it to come to pass. How good it is to know that other men and women of God experienced such feelings and went on to great success.

One of the things I love about the Bible is the fact that it does not hide the moments of crises through which the people of faith passed in former days. That's very important to me. If they had never struggled, I would wonder if I was normal or if I was spiritual enough to succeed.

But the characters of the Bible are never wooden, make-believe characters. They're real men and woman with real problems and real moments of crisis. And they have passions and feelings and viewpoints and opinions just like we do.

There are four things that can cause us to quit, and we must learn to avoid them. All of us fall into one of these four categories.

Problems Can Make Us Want to Quit

The most common thing that can cause us to want to quit is problems. Sometimes the situations of life cause many problems for us, and it is the devil's objective to keep our lives filled with as many of them as possible. He wants us to have so many problems that we begin to lose faith and trust in God.

178

Learning to Avoid Quitting

There are problems at work, problems at home, problems in your marriage, problems with the children, and on and on it goes. If you have enough of them, it becomes overwhelming.

There are problems and then there are *problems*. Some problems are so serious and so seemingly difficult to resolve that they can get on the inside of you. And that, again, makes you want to quit.

People Can Make You Want to Quit

People can be problems, and problems with people sometimes make you want to quit. The devil has a way of placing certain troublesome people in your life, in just such a way as to make you miserable. Some people seem to be called to annoy you. When you see them coming, you just want to run the other way.

If the enemy doesn't use problems to make you quit, he'll use people to make you quit. And if he doesn't use people to make you quit, he'll use position to make you want to quit.

Position Can Make You Want to Quit

Sometimes your position in life can make you want to quit. You know you're saved, you know you're sanctified, you know you love God, but it gets on your nerves that while you're trying to live right some people who don't even seem to be thinking about God are excelling. They're pulling ahead of you, and they don't even deserve to be blessed. They're pulling ahead so fast that it makes you look like you're standing still.

But before you think about giving up, before you decide to throw in the towel, hear what the Bible says:

Do not fret because of evildoers, nor be envious of the workers of iniquity. For they shall soon be cut down like the grass, and wither as the green herb. Trust in the LORD, and do good; dwell in the land, and feed on His faithfulness. Delight yourself also in the LORD, and He shall give you the desires of your heart. Commit your way to the LORD, trust also in Him, and He shall bring it to pass. He shall bring forth your righteousness as the light, and your justice as the noonday. Rest in the LORD, and wait patiently for Him; do not fret because of him who prospers in his way, because of the man who brings wicked schemes to pass. Cease from anger, and forsake wrath; do not fret—it only causes harm. For evildoers shall be cut off; but those who wait on the LORD, they shall inherit the earth.

Psalm 37:1–9

Don't allow anything about your present position to make you want to quit, for if God says something is yours, it's yours. Just because it's been delayed doesn't mean that it's been denied. Know what is yours and refuse to allow your current position in life to determine your position in Christ. Although it may look like everyone else in the world is going ahead of you, God always saves the best until last.

You can't quit now. It doesn't matter what your position is. God has made you a promise, and you're closer now than you've ever been to receiving it.

If you were not a person of faith, you would have given up a long time ago. If you were not clinging to the promise of God for your life, you would have been destroyed by this time. Hold on. Your day is coming. You can't quit now.

Perspective Can Make You Want to Quit

The enemy may have used problems against you, he may have used people, or he may have used position. If those don't work, he will use perspective. Satan has a way of making you see the worst side of things and never the best. I'm sure that everything is not the way you wish it were, but I can tell you that it could be a whole lot worse.

You ought to thank God for your problems, for there are people who are so much worse off than you are at the moment that they're wishing they could trade places with you. The devil wants you to complain about what you don't have, but you ought to reverse that and say, "Devil, I'm tired of complaining about what I don't have. I'm going to start thanking God for what I *do* have." That change of attitude will signal a change in everything else.

Your situation is not all that bad. It really isn't. And what is happening has not caught God by surprise. If God has allowed you to go through what you're going through, then He already knows the end result. He knows that if you're allowed to go through this, He will bring you out of it on the other side.

Some of us have been through so much that we can be assured that God hasn't brought us this far to abandon us now. When people look at you, they could never imagine all that you've been through, but in spite of it all, you're still here.

And the most amazing thing is that you still have your joy. You still have your peace. You still have your dance. You still have your praise. The devil can take whatever he wants, but he can't have our joy. That's our strength:

The joy of the LORD is your strength.

Nehemiah 8:10

You may not know how you're coming out of all this, but you will come out. You know the promise of God:

LIVING THE DREAM

And we know that all things work together for good to those who
love God, to those who are the called according to His purpose.
Romans 8:28

You can't quit. You're too close to the finish line. You've come too far to turn back now. Make up your mind. Stay strong and see if the finish line is not just ahead.

You should have been dead a long time ago. That bullet should have hit you. But God spared your life.

As we have seen, Elijah was a man of God and a prophet. He had just challenged four hundred and fifty of the prophets of Baal and put them to shame openly. Afterwards he had killed them. He was so powerful that he had confronted King Ahab himself (see 1 Kings 18). So he had just come from a major victory, but now he was suddenly running for his life. One moment he was rejoicing over his great victory, and not long afterward he was saying he wanted to die. What could make a mighty man like that want to quit on life? There are three things that we see in Elijah's case that we can all do to avoid quitting.

Don't Digest Discouragement

Bad news has a way of getting to a person. The enemy knows that, so he delights in sending you bad news. That's what happened to Elijah when he received the message from Jezebel. But this news would not have been so devastating if he had just refused to accept it.

You see, he not only received the words of discouragement (swallowing them), but he also digested them. What he didn't realize was that the devil was using Jezebel. She had sent a messenger to him to threaten his life. All of her prophets had been killed, so she felt threatened.

Learning to Avoid Quitting

Most of the people who are trying to hold you down are down themselves. When they're trying to hold you back, it's because they see the potential on the inside of you for you to have what they can't have. Be careful whom you listen to, for if you keep company with the wrong people, they will give you all kinds of discouraging words.

If you listen to people, they will cause you to back up on what God has promised you. Check your company; misery loves company. And people who are down want to keep you down too. Don't digest discouragement.

Let me ask the question: Whose report will you believe? Will you believe the report of your boss, your job, and your paycheck? Or will you believe that God can prepare a table for you in the very presence of your enemies? Will you believe that God can use people to bless you who don't even know you or like you? Will you believe that this will happen without them even knowing why they're blessing you? Trust God, and watch it happen.

It doesn't matter what things look like now; they're about to change.

One of the reasons that God has to bring you through what you're going through now is that you have opened your mouth and told people that He would. And He can't be left looking bad. He will come through for His name's sake, for in a very real sense, His name is on the line.

Refuse to digest discouragement, and don't let bad news affect you. When you have prayed about something and the situation seems to be getting worse, that's the time to shout because your prayers are working. This is your time.

You may well have sinned in the past, and the devil will tell you that what you are experiencing is because of your sin and that you can't be forgiven. But you have the promise of God:

LIVING THE DREAM

If we confess our sins, He is faithful and just to forgive us our sins and to cleanse us from all unrighteousness.

1 John 1:9

This promise is still yours because God said so. Praise Him for it.

Don't Compete or Compare

If you're going to avoid quitting, first don't digest discouragement, and second don't compete or compare. Elijah made the critical mistake of comparing himself with his father (see verse 4). Where did that come from? We know nothing about Elijah's father, but Elijah himself was a great man. What did his comparison to his father have to do with anything? Surprisingly, though, this is the mind-set of many people today. They are constantly comparing themselves with others. God does not expect you to do better than or equal to someone else; He only wants you to be your best.

We're so busy competing and so busy comparing that we become bound by this mentality. Then we start acting rashly. As soon as another person begins to make it to the top, we want to reach up and pull him or her down. But when God is blessing your neighbor, that isn't the time for you to begin to hate him. That's the time for you to rejoice. If God is blessing your neighbor, then that means He's part of your neighborhood.

I want to see you blessed because, if you get yours, that lets me know that mine must be on the way. I want you to get your breakthrough, I want the door to open for you, and it will. Don't compete and don't compare.

We're so busy trying to outdo somebody else, trying to out-dress somebody else, trying to do whatever is necessary to impress others, that we go to extremes and do ourselves more harm than good. Stop trying to impress people and concentrate on pleasing God. You don't have time to spend impressing others.

After Elijah had sat for a while under the tree comparing himself with his father and wanting to die, he fell asleep. And while he slept, something wonderful began to happen:

> Then as he lay and slept under a broom tree, suddenly an angel touched him, and said to him, "Arise and eat." Then he looked, and there by his head was a cake baked on coals, and a jar of water. So he ate and drank, and lay down again. And the angel of the LORD came back the second time, and touched him, and said, "Arise and eat, because the journey is too great for you." So he arose, and ate and drank; and he went in the strength of that food forty days and forty nights as far as Horeb, the mountain of God.
>
> 1 Kings 19:5–8

If you will stop your pity party long enough to see what God is doing, He will meet all of your needs. He supplied miraculously for the prophet, and he had strength enough for the next forty days.

You would think that Elijah would have been encouraged by now, but when he arrived at Horeb he went into a cave and God had to speak to him again:

> And there he went into a cave, and spent the night in that place; and behold, the word of the LORD came to him, and He said to him, "What are you doing here, Elijah?" So he said, "I have been very zealous for the LORD God of hosts; for the children of Israel have forsaken Your covenant, torn down Your altars, and killed Your prophets with the sword. I alone am left; and they seek to take my life." Then He said, "Go out, and stand on the mountain before the LORD." And behold, the LORD passed by, and a

great and strong wind tore into the mountains and broke the rocks in pieces before the LORD, but the LORD was not in the wind; and after the wind an earthquake, but the LORD was not in the earthquake; and after the earthquake a fire, but the LORD was not in the fire; and after the fire a still small voice. So it was, when Elijah heard it, that he wrapped his face in his mantle and went out and stood in the entrance of the cave. Suddenly a voice came to him, and said, "What are you doing here, Elijah?" And he said, "I have been very zealous for the LORD God of hosts; because the children of Israel have forsaken Your covenant, torn down Your altars, and killed Your prophets with the sword. I alone am left; and they seek to take my life."

1 Kings 19:9–14

Elijah was in a cave, and some of you are in a cave too. You're there competing and comparing and digesting discouragement, and I hear God saying to you, "What are you doing down there, as good as I've been to you? You have allowed people stop your progress. You have allowed people who don't like you to cause you to want to quit. You'd better get up because what I promised you is still yours."

It's not time to be sitting pouting. It's time to get up and move. Stop the pity party, and start being who God called you to be.

"What are you doing here?" the Lord asked Elijah, and Elijah had his same practiced answer. He was the only one still serving God. This was a terrible exaggeration.

Don't Exaggerate; Rather, Evaluate

Don't be guilty of what Elijah did. He began to exaggerate, suggesting that he was the only one trying to serve God, the only righteous person left, and now someone was trying to take his life.

Learning to Avoid Quitting

Satan loves nothing more than to confuse your mind and to cloud your perspective. You're going through something. That much is true, but others are too. I know that you feel all alone. I've experienced it myself.

Every time my back was up against the wall, it seemed to be just God and I. When I examined that, I found that it was not such a bad thing. When other people left me alone, then I could hear God's voice.

It's always been God and I. As much as I appreciate the prayers of others, I don't really need them because I can always pray for myself. That's the only way I can get to heaven.

Stop the pity party and turn it into a victory celebration. Rather than lament your losses, start praising God for every one of your enemies. Praise Him for those who smiled in your face and stabbed you in the back at the same time. If you hadn't had so many enemies, you might have become proud. But because you knew that many people wanted to see you fail, it made you walk straight. It made you live right.

As for me, I can't quit. I can't turn around. God's been too good to me. They might lock me up and throw away the key, but I won't stop praising God until I come out of there. I know that if I trust God, He'll work it out.

As you learn to avoid quitting, you place yourselves further along the road to *Living the Dream.*

LIVING THE DREAM

Chapter Fourteen

LEARNING TO REALIZE THAT IT'S WORTH THE FIGHT

And he arose that night and took his two wives, his two female servants, and his eleven sons, and crossed over the ford Jabbok. He took them, sent them over the brook, and sent over what he had. Then Jacob was left alone; and a Man wrestled with him until the breaking of day. Now when He saw that He did not prevail against him, He touched the socket of his hip; and the socket of Jacob's hip was out of joint as He wrestled with him. And He said, "Let Me go, for the day breaks." But he said, "I will not let You go unless You bless me!" So He said to him, "What is your name?" He said, "Jacob." And He said, "Your name shall no longer be called Jacob, but Israel; for you have struggled with God and with men, and have prevailed."

Genesis 32:22–28

Elijah was not the only Bible character to struggle with discouragement. They all had to face this fight. Jacob experienced a literal wrestling match with an angel, and from his experience we can learn many important things about our own struggle. The most important one is that it's worth the fight.

Jacob's early years were spent in conflict with his twin brother Esau. In the end, through premeditated trickery, Jacob wrestled both the birthright and the favored blessing from his brother. But as a result of his dishonesty, he was forced to flee from his home and live elsewhere for many years. This scheming and conniving proved to be part of Jacob's character. In fact, his very name meant supplanter, or trickster, and he certainly was one.

The amazing part of the story is that Jacob tried in all that he did to please God and that God continually blessed him—regardless of his personal failures. God is God, after all, and He can do that if He wants to. There is no searching of His understanding:

His understanding is unsearchable.

Isaiah 40:28

Jacob was eventually reconciled with his brother, with God, and with himself. The trials that led him to this point came at the hand of his own extended family members, not from an outside force. The people within his family caused him his greatest problems.

Now, he who tricked his brother and his father, found himself tricked by his uncle (who also happened to be his father-in-law). My mother often told me something as I was growing up that did not make sense to me until years later. Now I know that it is a well known phrase, and one that is used often. She said, "What goes around comes around." Now I understand what it means. Jacob learned it the hard way.

Learning to Realize That It's Worth the Fight

Because Jacob had tricked others, he himself became the victim of trickery.

After he fled from his home, Jacob went to a place called Haran with the hope of finding a wife. He stopped at a well, much as the servant of his grandfather, Abraham, had done many years before. There a young lady caught his eye.

Her name was Rachel, she was his uncle Laban's daughter, and she was so beautiful and so charming that she immediately captivated him. That same day, Jacob told his uncle that he would be willing to stay in his house and serve him seven years for the privilege of marrying his daughter Rachel.

Rachel must have been very desirable for Jacob to have made such a promise for her. Seven years is a long time, and that was a lot to pay for a wife. But good things are worth what you pay for them, and Jacob seemed to know it.

The seven years passed, and I'm sure Jacob felt it seemed like just a short time, since he was anticipating a lifetime with the woman he loved. The moment arrived, the wedding was performed, and he retired to his bedchamber and consummated his marriage to the woman before him.

What a shock it must have been to wake up the next morning and discover that it was not Rachel whom he had married, but Leah, her older sister, someone whom he had not been physically attracted to at all! Leah had nice eyes, but it was Rachel who was beautiful in every way. Now he pulled back the covers, and there lay Leah.

Jacob must have been shocked, insulted, and outraged. He went immediately to Laban and asked how this thing could have happened. Well, Laban explained, it was customary not to give a younger daughter in marriage before an older daughter had been wed.

As angry as he was, there was not a lot that Jacob could do at that moment. He was a foreigner in this place, and he had no legal recourse. He told Laban that he didn't appreciate what he had done to him, but that he would serve another seven years, if only he could have Rachel, as he had originally been promised. Laban agreed. Now, Jacob was willing to work fourteen years for the woman of his dreams, and he did.

But this was just the first of many incidents in which Laban would outfox the fox and outmaneuver the trickster. In Laban, Jacob had met his match. If he was somewhat of a con artist, his Uncle Laban was his equal. Over the coming years, he would change Jacob's wages many times, and, in every other way—honest and dishonest—he sought an advantage over his son-in-law.

Just as Jacob had taken advantage of his father's poor eyesight, now his own eyes were blinded to the fact that he had the wrong woman in his bed on his wedding night. That's pretty bad. Just as he had taken advantage of his brother when he came in from the field weak and hungry, his father-in-law had now taken advantage of his youthful passions.

But in all of this Jacob had purpose and destiny, and he kept on going moving toward his dream. Likewise, no matter what may be happening in your life, you, too, have purpose and destiny. You're on the right road and you're making good time. Just keep going. Don't let anything stop you. It's worth the fight.

Because your purpose is not yet totally clear, you're not sure just how close you are to being where God wants you to be. My assignment in this book has been to let you know that God has never intended for you to live in exile and slavery. He wants you to achieve your intended purpose in life.

Right here on earth, God will fulfill every promise that He has made to every person because, as His Word declares, He never lies:

Learning to Realize That It's Worth the Fight

God is not a man, that He should lie, nor a son of man, that He should repent. Has He said, and will He not do? Or has He spoken, and will He not make it good?

Numbers 23:19

We just need to hang on a little while longer and to keep on walking, trusting, and depending on God for the final outcome. He will not fail us.

I promise you that if you do, in a matter of months, weeks, or even days, you will find yourself in your promised land living as you have never lived before, enjoying life like you've never enjoyed it before. It will be so much better than what you're currently experiencing that there will be no comparison.

Your testimony will soon be, "As I look back and see where the Lord has brought me from, I'm amazed." Everyone else will be amazed too.

I can tell you that He's brought me a very long way, and yet I sense that the best days are just ahead. God is ready to bless us as we've never, ever been blessed before.

Friend, your struggle, your fight, is just about over, and the devil is confused because he doesn't understand why you still have your joy, why you still have peace, why you still have a will to go on when people have done you so wrong.

You've been hit high, and you've been hit low, but something on the inside of you won't let you quit. You're determined to fight this fight to the finish, and what I am saying here is only a confirmation to what the Lord has been showing you personally. You've been sensing that your life is about to change for the better. You can't quit now. You're too close to turn back. Your promise is just down the street. Your breakthrough is just around the corner.

God is about to show His power on your behalf. This is your season.

That's why the devil has been attacking you like never before. But some of you feel just like I do, and just like the four Hebrews boys felt. Their tormentors could turn the heat up seven times hotter if they wanted, but those Hebrew boys still wouldn't bow down to their gods.

No wonder the enemy has fought you so! No wonder you've gone through so many difficult relationships! No wonder people have stabbed you in the back so many times. You're destined for greatness. You must be somebody important!

Some people already had you dead and buried. They were already throwing dirt on top of your casket. But just as they thought you were finished and were starting to walk away, you rose up from that place.

You've been pushed down so far that you have no place to go but up. Things can't get any worse; they have to get better. You're on your way to your purpose and destiny.

You know that you should still be in jail, and it wasn't the lawyer who got you out. It wasn't the judge. It was Almighty God Himself, and He has looked beyond your faults and seen your need. Now, you're on assignment for the Lord. You have a call on your life. You're no longer your own. You have to stay the course. It's worth the fight.

Jacob was on his way to purpose and destiny, and for many of us, in order to receive what Jacob received, we have to do what Jacob did. What was that? First, he arose and crossed over, and then he sent his family on ahead of him so that he could get alone with God.

Learning to Realize That It's Worth the Fight

Separate Yourself

The first step toward finding your purpose and destiny is to separate yourself. You have to do it.

Separate yourself from some things that hinder you. Separate yourself from some places where you shouldn't be going anymore. And separate yourself from some people who are not going where you're going.

Some of the people who participated in the previous season of your life will not be going on with you now. Many of the people smiling at you every day are not your friends. They're just trying to get what they can from you. Just as soon as you experience your breakthrough, you'll see what I mean.

As we have seen, they're not your real friends. They may not want to leave you, but you have to separate yourself from them so that you can find your true destiny. *"Jacob was left alone."*

If someone were to ask you who your best friends are, you wouldn't know what to answer. Many of you don't even have a best friend, and that's not always a bad thing. Why have you suddenly found yourself alone? Because eagles never fly in groups like buzzards do. Geese and wild turkeys fly together, but eagles fly alone. And in this season, because of where you're about to go and what you're about to get, you'd better get used to being alone.

Stop feeling like you need a man or a woman to complete you. Just take yourself to dinner. In this next season, it will be just you and Jesus. Separate yourself.

You should be glad that you don't fit in with the crowd. You ought to be glad that when you walk up, people start acting differently. Jacob was left alone, and sometimes you will be left alone too.

I know that it's sometimes hard to be alone, but I believe that Jacob had to be alone. For what God was about to do in his life, other people would have just gotten in the way. With where God was taking him, people would have been a hindrance.

Anyway, you can't hear God if you're constantly listening to everyone else around you. It's time to separate yourself.

Be Committed to Change

After Jacob was left alone, he began to pray, and the Bible says that a Man appeared, looking like an angel, and began wrestling with Jacob. They wrestled until the break of day. What an exhausting wresting match that must have been!

At some point in the match, the Man injured Jacob's thigh. This injury was so serious that it affected Jacob's stride for the rest of his life. In that moment, the pain must have been intense. I can imagine that tears streamed down Jacob's face as he fought relentlessly on. He was hurting, but he refused to let it stop him. He was committed to change.

Do you need some change in your life? Well, it's worth the fight. Stay committed, and your answer will come. When you get to the other side, you will realize that it has been worth every tear you've shed, every lonely night you've spent, and every hardship you had to go through along the way. Stay the course.

Jacob was so exhausted and injured that he was practically reduced to one good leg, but still he fought on. The night deepened, and he fought on. Then the night passed, the daylight began to come again, and still he fought on. Now the sun was coming up, and he had not yet given up. All the while, he apparently didn't even know whom he was fighting.

Learning to Realize That It's Worth the Fight

Eventually the angel realized that Jacob was not yielding, and he said to him, "Let me go."

Jacob was not about to let him go. "Not until you bless me," he responded. This encounter had caused him serious pain, and he was not about to let go of it until he received what he needed.

Hold on, friend. Your answer is on the way.

Your heart may be hurting, and you may be in serious pain. Your bills may be backed up or you may not know where your next meal is coming from. Hold on. Be committed to change.

You may have been hurt by church members, and those you have done the most for may have let you down. But hold on.

Your spouse may be threatening to leave you, but hold on. The Lord will always be by your side. Remain committed to change.

What was it that enabled Jacob to hold on under such drastic circumstances? We find the answer to that in his prayer to God recorded earlier:

> *Deliver me, I pray, from the hand of my brother, from the hand of Esau; for I fear him, lest he come and attack me and the mother with the children. For You said, "I will surely treat you well, and make your descendants as the sand of the sea, which cannot be numbered for multitude."*
>
> Genesis 32:11–12

Jacob is putting God in remembrance of the promise He made him. If God said that He would bless him exceedingly and multiply his seed and make them *"as the sand of the sea,"* then Jacob had to hold on. He couldn't quit.

If you don't have a promise to cling to, it might be easy to give up, but when you're determined to begin *Living the Dream*, you simply cannot give up. You have to keep fighting.

LIVING THE DREAM

Some of you know what God has promised you, even though sometimes it looks like it will never come to pass. And you can give up on it. But you also can do what Jacob did. Put the Lord in remembrance of His promise.

When your bills are due and there is no money to pay them, you can go to God in prayer and remind Him that He said:

And my God shall supply all your need according to His riches in glory by Christ Jesus.

Philippians 4:19

When your body is racked with pain and there seems to be no relief, you can remind the Lord that He said:

Who Himself bore our sins in His own body on the tree, that we, having died to sins, might live for righteousness—by whose stripes you were healed.

1 Peter 2:24

When someone is smiling in your face and stabbing you in the back, you can remind God of His promise:

"No weapon formed against you shall prosper, and every tongue which rises against you in judgment you shall condemn. This is the heritage of the servants of the LORD, and their righteousness is from Me," says the LORD.

Isaiah 54:17

This doesn't mean that no one will try to do your harm; rather, it means that their attempts will not prosper.

When you understand what God has promised you (as Jacob did in verse 12), it will make you hold on (as he did in verse 24). Your miracle is on the way, and you've come through the worst of your trials. Don't give up now. Things are about to change for you. In fact, everything is about to change for you.

For many of you, your income is about to change. For some of you, your address is about to change. For many, your car is about to change. And that's just the beginning of the many changes the Lord will make in your life—if you let Him.

Conform to a Clean Confession

Right in the middle of this terrible fight, the angel had the nerve to ask Jacob what his name was. At that point, what difference did it make? They had been locked in deadly combat for hours already. Who cared what his name was?

But Jacob was on this way to fulfilling his dream; he was on his way to purpose and destiny. He was about to receive the greatest breakthrough he had ever experienced in his life.

Some of you are right where Jacob was at that moment. You've been in the fight, and you're wounded and in pain, but sill you're fighting on. Bills are due, and you're not sure what to do about it, but you're fighting on, determined not to let go until you have been blessed.

Your next miracle, your next breakthrough, is so important and so dynamic that it will not come to you easily. You'll have to fight for it. It will come on the heels of disappointment, difficulty, and pain. But you're close now, so don't give up. Don't stop fighting.

The angel asked Jacob what his name was because a name revealed character in those days. It revealed who you were, the real you. So now, Jacob—the supplanter, the trickster, the con artist—was nearing change, and he decided to be brutally honest with himself. The reason some of us can't get our breakthrough is because we refuse to be honest. We can't stop pointing the finger at other people long enough to see where we have erred.

We need to say, "It's me, it's me, Lord. I'm the one who's standing in need of prayer."

Jacob could have said, "I'm Isaac's son and Abraham's grandson," because he was. But this time he had to be honest. He was Jacob, the deceiver, and he could no longer deny who and what he was. He could no longer deny that most of troubles he had experienced he had brought on himself through his own actions.

Now Jacob was finally right where God wanted him to be, and He was ready to bless him:

And He said, "Your name shall no longer be called Jacob, but Israel; for you have struggled with God and with men, and have prevailed."

Genesis 32:28

The name Jacob means "deceiver," but the name Israel means "God prevails." This man was no longer Jacob; he was now Israel. He was no longer the trickster, the supplanter, the con man; he was now called by a new name.

God is about to make that same type of dramatic change in your life too. When He's done with you, you won't even recognize yourself. Now, the things that other people called you, they won't call you anymore. You're a changed person, and God is giving you a changed name.

You have been borrowers, but you're about to become lenders. You've been broke, but you're about to live in abundance. You've lived in pain and suffering, but you're about to move into healing and health.

Learning to Realize That It's Worth the Fight

There are those who will try to drag up the past and pull you back into it, but if they keep looking at what you used to be, they'll miss what you're about to become. God is about to change you dramatically.

When you come out of your fight, you'll discover on the other side of your breakthrough why you've gone through so much torment. You're a hero. You're an overcomer. You're a conqueror.

God wants to give you a ministry greater than anything you've seen before. He wants to give you a business unlike any you've ever seen before. He wants to give you a husband or wife unlike any you've ever seen before. He wants to give you a church like none other you've ever seen before.

Oh, neighbor, it's worth the fight. Hang on and keep fighting until your blessing comes.

The Bible declares,

For I consider that the sufferings of this present time are not worthy to be compared with the glory which shall be revealed in us.

Romans 8:18

Your promised end is glorious, and it's worth waiting for. The Lords also has said,

But those who wait on the LORD shall renew their strength; they shall mount up with wings like eagles, they shall run and not be weary, they shall walk and not faint.

Isaiah 40:31

When I go to McDonald's, I like to order a Big Mac. But I like mine without cheese. So, every time I make an order, the lady tells me that it will take a little longer because it has to be specially made. If you have wondered why everyone else is getting their miracle ahead of you, let me tell you that it's because yours is special. It will take a little longer, but it will come. It won't be the warmed-over kind. It will be special order.

Learn to Live with Your Limp

After Jacob was changed to Israel, he was all new—except for his damaged hip and the limp it left him with. God allowed his injury to become permanent to always remind Israel where he had come from. It was something that he just had to learn to live with.

I can imagine that, although it was a nuisance, Israel was somehow proud of his battle scars. He probably looked forward to the moment when people would ask him, "Why do you walk like that?" Then he could tell them, and it would remind him all over again of how very far he had come in God.

Those battle scars represent how we got to where we are, and we must never forget them. When someone asks, "How did you get that?" be sure to tell them and to give God all the glory, all the honor, and all the praise.

God had prevailed in his life, but Jacob (now Israel) was still limping. Some might have seen that as a sign of weakness and failure, but Israel knew it to be a sign of victory and conquest. He, more than anyone else, knew how very far he had come and how much he owed to the Lord for having brought him that far. Each of us has a limp of some kind as well, something that reminds us of our encounter with the Lord.

But whatever others thought of Israel's limp, he didn't mind it himself. He was so blessed that he could live with a little limp. He had found his purpose and his destiny in life and was now *Living the Dream*. What did a little limp mean to him?

Learning to Realize That It's Worth the Fight

He had been patient through the process and had endured what he had to endure to get to where he was. Now, that was all that mattered. Now, the struggles were forgotten, the insults were behind him, and the wrongs done to him by Laban and others were fading memories. Now, all that mattered was that he had arrived. He was happy *Living the Dream*.

LIVING THE DREAM

Chapter Fifteen

SO, STOP FIGHTING
THE PROCESS

Therefore rejoice, O heavens, and you who dwell in them! Woe to the inhabitants of the earth and of the sea! For the devil has come down to you, having great wrath, because he knows that he has a short time.

Revelation 12:12

We're living in the one of the most critical and sensitive times in the history of the world. From these days onward, every second counts. Because of that, it's important that we not fight the process. If we want to see the finished product, we must allow the process to run its course.

Too often, when we have looked at others and admired what we saw, we were only seeing the finished product. We failed to see behind the scenes to what God had done in that person's life to bring it all to pass.

When a person is deemed to be successful, we somehow think that he just got there. But it doesn't happen that way. A long process is necessary in order to obtain greatness. That's why many of us have to go through what seems like hell on earth. We go through so many problems that we wonder where God is and just what He's doing in our lives.

All of this is part of the perfecting process. This is the means God has chosen to get you from where you are to where He wants you to be. You're not where He wants you to be yet, but you're on your way, and if you will allow the process to be completed, you will surely arrive at your destiny.

We think of David as king of Israel, of Joseph as prime minister of Egypt, and of Gideon as judge over his people, but we forget that David had to start out as a shepherd boy, Joseph had his start in a pit and a prison, and Gideon was once a very desperate and dispirited man.

For David, the pasture was part of the process that got him to the palace. For Joseph, being sold into slavery could not have been pleasant, but he kept his focus on his dream and prevailed. For Gideon, a wonderful change of thinking came about when someone spoke a positive word over his life—a word of destiny and purpose—and that enabled him to overcome adversity and move on to greatness.

We conveniently forget that these men were ostracized and criticized, and, in the case of both Joseph and David, were not even welcomed by their own families. It was not the gleaming crown that enabled David to write,

The Lord is my shepherd; I shall not want.

Psalm 23:1

So, Stop Fighting the Process

I will bless the LORD at all times; His praise shall continually be in my mouth. My soul shall make its boast in the LORD; the humble shall hear of it and be glad. Oh, magnify the LORD with me, and let us exalt His name together. I sought the LORD, and He heard me, and delivered me from all my fears.

Psalm 34:1–4

No, when we read those words, we're looking at the finished product, but it took some time and many trials for David to get to that coveted place of victory.

Right now, you're going through the process, and it seems like the devil is turning your world upside down. But God has it all under control, and what He has in mind is something very wonderful. You're right where He wants you, and it's all been part of the process.

When you finally arrive at your destination, you won't just have a title; you'll also have a testimony. Let the process continue to its glorious end.

Right at this moment, you're somewhere between where you've come from and where you're going, and you may think you're stuck in place. But you're not stuck in place at all. You're just in transition to greatness. God is doing something wonderful in your life. Accept it, and glory in it.

I cannot explain the reasons that God sometimes uses pain to get us to the next level, but He does. Then, after the pain is past, comes the pleasure. The pain is never pleasant, but when you know the promised future, you can endure it and come out on the other side of it whole.

Only in recent years did I begin to understand this text verse: *"The devil has come down to you, having great wrath, because he knows that he has a short time."* At first, I couldn't believe what God was showing me through this, but then it all began to make sense. Satan thinks that he's doing us a great disservice by tormenting us and testing us, but, in reality, God is using that old fool to bless us. His antics provide our training and testing grounds.

Now that we know this, much of what we have been experiencing makes perfect sense. We suffered unspeakable torments and couldn't understand why. We were tormented with thoughts of being punished for all of our past failures, of being not good enough for God's blessings, and even of missing out on heaven and eternal life. But those were all lies.

How wonderful to know that everything we have endured has had a purpose. We're not being punished; we're being perfected. We're not falling short of God's blessings; His blessings are revealed through adversity. We're not in danger of missing heaven; we have a great destiny both here and in the hereafter. Satan knows it, and that's why he has worked so hard against us.

We all have been victims of the devil's most effective weapon—deception (lies, deceit, being fooled, misled, trickery, half-truths). That's how he deals with us. The fact that the Bible says, *"All have sinned, and come short of the glory of God"* (Romans 3:23 KJV) proves that we all have been deceived at some point. Our sin is the result of having been deceived.

In reality, we're caught in the middle of a battle between God and the devil. The devil tries to use us to get back at God, but we're little more than pawns in his chess game. His greatest desire is to hurt God, and he accomplishes it by hurting the ones God loves.

Satan is able to control those who don't know Christ, and their end will be sad. But for those of you who are saved and know it, the devil has no effective way of bringing you down to hell. You may not be perfect yet, but if you're saved, that's your ticket to get into heaven. The blood of Jesus has washed you, purged you, and sealed you unto the day of redemption. What Satan opts to do in these cases is to bring as much of hell as possible to you. He does it because he's angry with God, and he does what he does well—with *"great wrath."*

What a fool he is. Doesn't he realize that he's helping us be overcomers? Doesn't he recognize that he's creating a situation in which God can show Himself strong on our behalf?

Just as what is happening to you is no accident, you're reading this book was no accident either. You're reading this on purpose, and your destiny is to have dominion, to rule, and to have an abundant life in the process. God did not intend for you to just barely get by. He destined you to an overflowing life. And you're almost there. Keep preparing for the palace, and your day will come.

I can only imagine what it felt like to David the first day he stood in the palace as king of Israel, to Joseph in his first day in office as prime minister of Egypt, or to Gideon his first day in office as judge over his people. Surely they must all three have marveled at what had brought them to that day. They could not have imagined that it would happen as it did. But they had endured the process and prepared for the palace. And now they were *Living the Dream.*

LIVING THE DREAM